"And You Shall Teach Them Diligently"

A Concise History of Jewish Education
in the United States
1776–2000

The Jewish Education Series:

"And You Shall Teach Them Diligently"

A Concise History of Jewish
Education in the United States
1776–2000

Gil Graff

The Jewish Theological Seminary of America

The publication of the Jewish Education Series
is made possible by the generous support
of Mr. Earle Kazis and the Kazis Publication Fund.

To Ari, Ilan, and Talia
and generations to follow

THE JEWISH
EDUCATION
SERIES

Contents

Acknowledgments

This work is an outgrowth of studies and experiences shaped by numerous individuals and institutions in the field of Jewish education. Though I have made every effort to offer a dispassionate account, I am by no means distant from the subject explored in these chapters. I take this opportunity to acknowledge with appreciation significant influences on my thinking about the issues and settings discussed in these pages.

That I was an enrollee-participant in many of the frameworks of Jewish education that had been developed in the United States by the mid-twentieth century owes much to choices made by my parents, Dr. Chaim and Senta Graff, to whom I express abiding thanks. I am indebted to Dr. Sheldon Dorph, whose professional leadership and educational vision in directing a Hebrew high school inspired me to consider training for a career in Jewish education. My interest in probing matters of Jewish history was sparked by Professor Isaiah Gafni and deepened by my dissertation adviser, the late Professor Amos Funkenstein, whose encouragement and support I recall with gratitude.

Since 1985, my professional activity has been anchored at the Bureau of Jewish Education of Greater Los Angeles. The staff and board of the BJE are continuing sources of education and inspiration, and I am privileged to work in such a creative and fertile environment. Neither the completion of my daily work nor the publication of this volume would be possible without the diligent, capable, and unstinting administrative support of Miriam Goldman, to whom I express great appreciation.

I acknowledge with thanks the counsel and friendship of the former executive director of the Bureau of Jewish Education, Dr. Emil Jacoby, who encouraged my continuing research and teaching. In 1990–91, I enjoyed a year's leave as a Jerusalem Fellow in Israel, where I benefited significantly from the mentorship of the late Professor Seymour Fox, a remarkable visionary in the field of Jewish education.

Since 1970, I have taught students in elementary school, high school, college, graduate school, rabbinical school, continuing education programs, and Elderhostel classes. From these interactions, I have learned a great deal. I acknowledge with thanks the students who have contributed to my ongoing education and am grateful to have been welcomed as part of the teaching faculty at many schools, institutions of higher learning, and synagogues—Conservative, Orthodox, Reconstructionist, and Reform—over these several decades.

My professional experiences as executive director of a large-city central agency for Jewish education have brought me into close contact with a broad range of Jewish educational institutions and the people who conduct them. Curious to understand how the ever-growing variety of Jewish educational frameworks in the United States came to be developed, I began researching the subject. During this exploration, I investigated the broad topic at two major archives of Jewish life in the United States: the archives of the American Jewish Historical Society in New York; and the American Jewish Archives in Cincinnati. The AJHS provided a summer research fellowship, for which I am appreciative. The staffs of both institutions were most helpful and accommodating, and I gratefully acknowledge their assistance.

It was my wife, Robin, herself a Jewish educator, who suggested that I turn my personal examination of the subject into a short volume that might be of interest to others. For her support of this project, including review of the work, and for so much more, I am daily thankful. In developing the manuscript, I shared drafts at various stages with Jonathan Sarna, Jeffrey Schein, Jack Wertheimer, Jonathan Woocher, and Michael Zeldin, each of whom very generously offered helpful comments. Needless to say, any shortcomings of this book—which, as I note in the introduction, is in the nature of a prolegomenon—are entirely my own.

When I was ready to prepare a draft for publication, I was fortunate to enjoy a summer as Visiting Scholar at the Oxford Centre for Hebrew and Jewish Studies. I am grateful to the Centre, whose Yarnton Manor estate provided a beautiful setting in which to write, and to the welcoming and helpful OCHJS staff. I express thanks as well to Harriet Weinreich, of the BJE, for her able proofreading of the product of these efforts. Last, but by no means least, I express my appreciation to JTS Jewish Education Series editor Barry Holtz, copyeditor Janice Meyerson, and the anonymous reviewers whose comments and counsel were so helpful in bringing this publication to fruition.

Robin and I, both beneficiaries of the Jewish educational opportunities created by those who preceded us, are blessed with three children—Ari, Ilan, and Talia—whose adult lives will be part of the next chapter in the history of Jewish education in the United States. It is my hope that, like their parents and grandparents—and generations before them—they will, in their unique ways, find meaning in Jewish living and learning. It is to them and to those who follow that this book is dedicated.

Introduction

" And you shall teach them [words of Torah: Jewish instruction]
diligently to your children" (Deut. 6:7). There is perhaps no
better mirror of the values of a community at any given time or place
than its choices in the domain of education. For millennia, in widely
scattered places, and under various conditions, Jews have instructed
their children concerning the teachings and practices of Jewish life, enabling them to negotiate their way as Jews.

Jonathan Sacks, chief rabbi of the United Hebrew Congregations of
the British Commonwealth, notes that in premodern societies, priests
held a virtual monopoly on literacy. The word "hieroglyphic," for example, means priestly script. Similarly, the double meaning of "clerical,"
referring both to clergy and clerks, hearkens to the Middle Ages, when
religious functionaries were the educated class. That all Israel is instructed to be a "kingdom of priests" (Exod. 19:6) bespeaks an educational imperative devolving on all members of Israelite society.[1]

The Jews' penchant for learning was recognized by those outside
their circle. A twelfth-century monk observed: "The Jews, out of their
zeal for God and their love of the Law, put as many sons as they have to
letters, that each may understand God's law. . . . A Jew, however poor, if
he had ten sons, would put them all to letters, not for gain, as the Christians do, but for the understanding of God's Law, and not only his sons
but his daughters."[2]

Though perhaps exaggerated to support the cleric's call for greater
attention to learning among the Christian faithful, the general observation was reflected in communal mechanisms for ensuring Jewish education, wherever Jews lived. In the United States of America—where
Jewish association was, and has remained, voluntary—the history of

1

Jewish education, from 1776 to 2000, reflects movement from individual responsibility for Jewish learning toward a greater communal stake in the provision of Jewish education. In addition, an ever-expanding array of modalities and frameworks of Jewish education has been developed on American soil. This work explores these phenomena in their historical context, providing background useful in understanding contemporary trends in Jewish education.

When, in 1776, representatives of the thirteen American colonies declared independence from England, 2,000 Jews were among the more than 3 million inhabitants of what came to be the United States. In the New World, the corporate structures that had defined Jewish existence in medieval societies never existed. Nonetheless, by 1776, five *kehillot kodesh*, synagogue-communities, had been established by Jews in the colonies, and limited means of transmitting the Jewish heritage were in evidence. In the ensuing centuries, migrations, first largely from German-speaking lands (1840–1870s), and later—chiefly, though by no means exclusively—from Eastern Europe (1880–1925), brought millions of Jews to the United States. New emphases and mechanisms of Jewish education emerged during these waves of immigration. The destruction of most of Europe's Jews, the relocation to the United States of European Jews who survived the *Shoah* (Holocaust), and the establishment of the State of Israel had, in turn, a significant impact on Jewish education in America.

By the beginning of the twenty-first century, American Jewry exceeded 5 million people. School-based Jewish educational programs were reaching nearly 80 percent of children aged six to seventeen.[3] Synagogues, day schools, supplementary religious schools, early childhood programs, day camps, residential summer camps, Israel experiences, youth groups, college campus–based programs, adult learning programs of short- and longer-term duration, Jewish community centers, colleges of Jewish studies, and rabbinical seminaries were but some of the frameworks within which Jewish education was conducted under Jewish auspices. University departments of Jewish studies were, likewise, an important venue of Jewish learning for many. As the first school year of the twenty-first century began, a noted researcher estimated that $2 billion a year was being spent to educate the 200,000 students enrolled in Jewish day schools. As for the cost of Jewish education in all its expressions in the United States, the researcher correctly observed that no clearinghouse for such information existed and that, in short, "no one knows."[4]

Each of the hundreds of Jewish educational institutions operating early in the twenty-first century depends upon cadres of professional educators, volunteer trustees, board members, financial supporters, students, and—most directly, in the case of children in early childhood through high school—parents. Jewish tradition teaches: "Know from where you come and where you are headed" (Avot 3:1). Yet, for many who are deeply involved in Jewish educational leadership—as professionals, volunteer leaders, and parents—the history of Jewish educational initiatives in the United States prior to their own life story is unknown and remains unexplored. For such individuals and for those who are preparing for careers in Jewish education or Jewish communal service, this work outlines the trends that have marked the course of Jewish educational developments in the United States, enabling the reader to better understand contemporary issues and opportunities.

Beyond addressing the interest of those who personally identify with the American Jewish subculture, examination of the educational currents that have characterized the Jewish experience in the United States offers an instructive case study in the role of education in the continuity of an ethnic-religious minority in America. Several years ago, I was interviewed by a South Korean television crew that was filming a story of how Jews in the United States have maintained cultural identity over the course of centuries, despite being a small minority group. The station did not err in imagining that education is a significant part of this phenomenon.

In an article on the importance of historical inquiry, Michael Zeldin, dean of the Rhea Hirsch School of Education at Hebrew Union College, observes: "Histories of education can help policy makers in education transcend the present moment and see beyond today's immediate issues to the enduring qualities and values represented by policy alternatives. They can provide perspective on the relationship of actions to aims and purposes. . . . [T]he questions that are raised may indeed be changed when questions are seen as part of a larger saga."[5] While looking at the past cannot yield definitive conclusions about the present, let alone the future, it can provide a context within which to more fully—and perhaps more effectively—reflect upon current issues.

Surprisingly, there have been few efforts to chronicle the history of Jewish education in this country. A recently published volume, *The Education of Jews and the American Community: 1840 to the New Millennium,* is a posthumously released revision of Eduardo Rauch's doctoral dissertation (Harvard, 1978), concentrating on the period 1840–1920.[6]

The most complete treatment of the subject is a 1969 collection of six historical essays edited by Judah Pilch, titled *A History of Jewish Education in America*.[7]

In the same year that the Pilch volume appeared, Lloyd Gartner edited a book of documents relating to the history of Jewish education in the United States. In an introductory essay, Gartner provides a helpful overview of two centuries of educational currents and includes a partial list of bibliographical references.[8] Nearly thirty years later, the eminent historian of American Jewry Jonathan Sarna published an article in which he surveyed a number of themes in the history of Jewish education in the United States. Sarna laments the inattention hitherto given to this subject, particularly by those planning educational responses to continuity. Sarna suggests that "by carefully studying that history . . . we would be in a much better position than we are now to build securely for the future."[9] Sarna's *American Judaism* (2004) comprehensively explores the history of Jewish American religious life but does not undertake a comprehensive look at the history of Jewish education.[10]

In 2002, Jonathan Krasner, a student of Sarna's, wrote a doctoral dissertation that is a significant contribution to the work of historical inquiry into aspects of Jewish education in the United States.[11] Krasner explored the textbooks published for use in Jewish schools from approximately 1880 to 1980, analyzing the worldview they reflected and the messages they sought to convey. While schools are but one vehicle of Jewish education, and textbooks—to the degree that they are utilized— are filtered by teachers and students, Krasner's analysis provides a penetrating look at a century of development in a key domain of the explicit educational curriculum of Jewish schools.[12]

In 1996, an extensive bibliography of Jewish education in the United States was published. The compiler and editor, Norman Drachler, noted that "data about Jewish education in the United States is spread over a multitude of publications."[13] Drawing upon diverse sources, the present historical survey aims to concisely convey the key issues and to describe some of the personalities and institutions that have been at the core of Jewish education in the United States, from 1776 to the beginning of the twenty-first century.

Lawrence Cremin aptly defines "education" as "the deliberate, systematic and sustained effort to transmit, evoke or acquire knowledge, attitudes, values, skills or sensibilities as well as any outcomes of that effort."[14] Over the centuries, there has been a proliferation of settings and mechanisms for engaging participants in Jewish education of a "deliberate, systematic" sort. There has been, as well, considerable movement from the view of Jewish education as exclusively a matter of individual or family responsibility in the direction of recognizing a broader Jewish communal stake in the provision of Jewish education. These two dimensions of expanding notions of Jewish education are central to this work.

This introductory survey of the history of Jewish education in the United States is, by no means, the last word on the rich world of educators, creative educational strategies, instructional frameworks and materials, regional and generational and societal issues, or the conflicts that have influenced learners and teachers. In-depth studies of these topics, like those of gender issues, church-state considerations, various Jewish subcultures, particular disciplines of study, and the leaders and Jewish rank and file who have shaped and experienced Jewish education in America, remain to be produced. The primary focus of the present work is on the educational frameworks conceived and implemented at various junctures. Among the questions addressed are: Why were these particular frameworks developed? How were they implemented? By whom were they created? For whom were they designed? Who participated? While there is some anecdotal information about the learning that took place in the various settings, it is a subject requiring far greater study. By concisely providing basic knowledge of the history of Jewish education in the United States, this prolegomenon presents a context for understanding the rich variety of twenty-first-century Jewish educational currents and institutions—an understanding that may better equip successive generations "to build securely for the future." While there are notes and references to scholarly materials for those interested in a more complete read of areas of special interest to them, the body of the work is intended for the general reader.

It is my view that Jewish education should be seen as an organic whole, encompassing the many frameworks and venues in which it is experienced. I have chosen, therefore, to organize this narrative as a chronological account of multiple and generally related developments, rather than treating independently the history of various educational structures. In this way, the reader will be able to locate such institutions as Sunday schools, day schools, religious supplementary schools, rabbinical schools, Hebrew teachers' colleges, youth groups, camps, Hillel campus organizations, early childhood programs, Jewish community centers, adult education, family education, Israel experience programs, and other educational phenomena within their historical setting. Each chapter of the American Jewish experience must be understood in the broader context of the particular historical period, and trends in American education in successive eras are accordingly referenced. Moreover, the beginning of a new wave of immigration—for example, the arrival of millions of Eastern European Jews—does not close the chapter of those who came earlier. The interplay of newer currents and existing frameworks is part of the rich history of American Jewish education.

A note of explanation of the periodization utilized is in order. During the early national period (until 1840), Jewish population in the United States grew from 2,000 to 15,000, primarily through immigration. Jewish education was considered a matter of family, rather than communal, responsibility, and private tutors were the principal agents of religious instruction.

The period 1840–80 saw an explosion in Jewish population, from 15,000 to 250,000, resulting, in the main, from a major current of immigration from German-speaking lands, of which Jews were a part. Taking part in the national, westward movement, Jews settled and established congregations in emerging centers in the midwestern and western United States. In addition to initiating part-time frameworks of religious education, German Jews created dozens of day schools in the 1840s and 1850s. Acculturation, combined with the efforts of Reform rabbinic leadership, furthered Reform institutional growth, and, in 1875, the nation's first enduring rabbinical school—Hebrew Union College—was established in Cincinnati. By the 1870s, for reasons explained in Chapter 2, American Jews embraced public education, and all the day schools that had been initiated earlier closed their doors. The "Sabbath School" was, for a time, the ascendant Jewish instructional framework for children.

The massive wave of Jewish immigration to the United States beginning in the 1880s, mostly from Eastern Europe, brought a proliferation of *hadarim* (one-room "schools" conducted by private tutors) and of Talmud Torah (communal, supplementary) schools. At the same time, more traditional rabbinical academies were launched, along with a small number of new day schools. For the most part, Eastern European Jewish immigrants saw in the public school system a welcome opportunity for advancement and integration into American life. The importance of the year 1910—by which time American Jewry numbered 2 million—in periodizing the history of Jewish education in the United States lies in the establishment of the Bureau of Jewish Education by the New York Kehillah. This act was significant in the establishment of

Jewish education as a communal concern, not merely a matter of private or familial responsibility.

Over the period 1910–45, United States Jewry gradually—and then abruptly—emerged as the preeminent Jewish community in the world. This period was of particular significance in the institutional development of Jewish education. Bureaus of Jewish Education were established in many cities. Youth groups, community centers, summer camps, Jewish college campus organizations, foundation schools for children aged three to eight, and day schools were established; and congregation-sponsored afternoon schools supplanted Talmud Torah community schools as primary frameworks of Jewish education for children. The Depression took a significant toll on institutions of Jewish learning; yet it was in the 1930s and early 1940s that an influx of refugees, including individuals and groups deeply committed to intensive Jewish education, arrived in the United States. The impact of this relocation was to be keenly felt within a generation.

With the end of the war, the United States experienced a major resurgence of church/synagogue affiliation. In this climate, suburbanization and the creation of new neighborhoods meant the establishment of new synagogues, schools, and Jewish community centers. A further transplantation of tens of thousands of Jewish immigrants represented a cultural booster shot for American Jewry; awareness of the magnitude and horror of the Holocaust, combined with pride in the newly established State of Israel, contributed to heightened Jewish identity. The baby boom saw annual enrollment of students in Jewish schools, kindergarten through twelfth grade, approach 600,000 by the early 1960s. The ethnic pride of the late 1960s and 1970s made subcultural identification acceptable, even desirable. American Jews, it seemed, were achieving full integration into American life, while retaining a Jewish distinctiveness.

By the mid-1970s, however, there was considerable alarm among those concerned with Jewish survival in the United States. The National Jewish Population Survey of 1971 disclosed that 31 percent of Jews were intermarrying—up from 7 percent in the 1950s. Many Americans, including groups in which Jews were quite active, had been indifferent to the plight of Israel on the brink of the June 1967 war, and the Yom Kippur War of 1973 served as a reminder of Israel's vulnerability. Moreover, widely quoted doctoral dissertations from the University of Chicago and Harvard in 1975 and 1976[15] concluded that Jewish learning for Jewish living required more aggregate hours of Jewish education than virtually all those who did attend Jewish schools were receiving. Assessing the realities of American Jewish life, sociologist Charles Liebman, in a seminal work published in 1973, *The Ambivalent American Jew*, concluded that the dream of integration into American society and meaningful survival as Jews, as conceived to that point, was an unlikely possibility.[16] Whereas for generations, Jews had looked to Jewish education as a means of transmitting the tools for Jewish living, many now looked to Jewish education as a mechanism for answering the question "Why be Jewish?"

The closing generation of the twentieth century saw a proliferation of Jewish educational initiatives aimed at addressing the perceived challenge of Jewish continuity in the United States. The magnitude of this challenge was reflected in the 1990 National Jewish Population Survey, which indicated an intermarriage rate of 52 percent and a "flat" Jewish population at 5.5 million people, despite significant immigration from the former USSR and Iran. A reinvigorated day school movement, Birthright Israel trips, a strengthening of Hillel (college campus) foundations, Jewish educational partnerships between American Jewish communities and Israeli counterparts, and increased engagement of philanthropic foundations in promoting Jewish "renaissance and renewal" were elements of late-twentieth-century response. This historical look at the development of Jewish education in the United States ends with the findings of the National Jewish Population Survey of 2000–2001.

The saga of Jewish education in the United States remains dynamic in the early years of the twenty-first century. Such issues as public—or nonsectarian private—education versus Jewish day school education and the place of Hebrew in American Jewish education have been part of an ongoing debate spanning many generations. Universalism or particularism, accommodation or resistance to prevailing cultural norms, and emphasis on the peoplehood/community or religious/denominational dimension of the ethnic church that is Judaism are among the recurring themes in the history of American Jewish education. While Jewish educational developments are not entirely linear, the motifs of heightened communal engagement in the provision of Jewish education and an expanding array of Jewish educational frameworks are evident throughout the period surveyed, and these developments are integral to each chapter of this history.

The next chapter of Jewish education in the United States is yet to be written, and historians take to heart the Talmudic dictum that prophetic insight—at least in recent millennia—has been accorded exclusively to children and fools. This work does, however, close with some thoughts on current and emerging directions in Jewish education in the United States. With the past as a springboard and a vision of the future as inspiration, it remains for each generation to "teach them diligently."

CHAPTER ONE
Jewish Education in the Early National Period, 1776–1840

As the American colonies declared their independence on July 4, 1776, 2,000 Jews were among the more than 3 million Americans about to launch a new national saga. Nearly half of these Jews were associated with one of the five congregations established during the colonial period in New York (Shearith Israel), Newport (Jeshuat Israel), Savannah (Mickve Israel), Philadelphia (Mikveh Israel), and Charleston (Beth Elohim), each of which followed the Sephardic ritual.[17] The early Jewish colonists were primarily of Spanish and Portuguese ancestry, stemming from ex-Marrano or Western Sephardi stock.[18] They maintained religious faith, kinship connections, and an affinity for Jewish ceremonies, but their knowledge of classical Jewish sources was, at best, limited. Though by 1720, Ashkenazim constituted a majority of the small, colonial American Jewish population, the first congregation to follow the Ashkenazic rite—Rodeph Shalom, in Philadelphia—was not established until 1802.

Jacob Rader Marcus, the great twentieth-century historian of American Jewry, describes colonial Jewish life:

> When the Jew left Europe, he left behind him . . . the all-pervasive authority of the Jewish community. . . . Religious controls were inevitably relaxed here. There was much less concern about observance and ritual. The individual was far freer to do as he pleased. He could if he wished—and most commonly he did wish—pay much less attention to the rabbinic learning which, for a thousand years had been the leitmotif of European Jewish life. The new American Jew, who was beginning to emerge on the Colonial scene, much preferred to be a successful

merchant than a talmudic scholar. . . . If he finally settled in a Colonial village, it was usually only a matter of time before he married a Christian and permitted his wife to rear his children as she thought fit.[19]

Indeed, of all known marriages involving Jews in the United States from 1776 to 1840, nearly 30 percent were intermarriages, and Jewish learning was at a very low ebb.[20]

Throughout the colonial and early national periods, congregational life was led by volunteer trustees and non-ordained religious functionaries; no rabbi settled in the United States until 1840.[21] Jews acquired burial grounds, established mechanisms for aiding the poor, and built synagogues for public worship, but they did not regard education as a communal responsibility. Tutoring in the mechanical reading of Hebrew, prayers, and limited instruction in Torah—primarily reading and translating—was provided for a fee, most commonly by independent teachers. Congregations would sometimes contract with an instructor to provide education to children of the poor.

Ezra Stiles, a Protestant clergyman who was later to serve as president of Yale University, attended religious services at Newport's Jewish congregation from time to time. A 1770 entry in Stiles's diary noted that the son of the deceased Moses Lopez led the Friday evening service in Hebrew. In a 1773 entry, Stiles related that Jacob Rodrigues Rivera's young son, eight or nine years of age, read the prophetic selection—in Hebrew—on the first day of Shavuot.[22]

That knowledge of Hebrew was, on the whole, rudimentary, was expressed by Hazzan (non-ordained "minister") Isaac Pinto of Shearith Israel in New York, who translated prayer-book passages into English in 1761 because Hebrew was "imperfectly understood by many, by some not at all."[23] Nonetheless, colonial congregations provided companionship with fellow Jews, a place to worship when one was so moved, a place to celebrate life-cycle events, access to kosher meat for those who sought it, assurance of proper burial, and the opportunity to give or receive charity. Moreover, the Jewish congregation was, for Jews, a parallel of sorts to the established churches that were a part of eighteenth-century American life.[24] Though ritual practices were observed by individual Jews haphazardly, the congregation operated in accordance with traditional norms. For example, Philadelphia's Mikveh Israel employed a "Shabbos goya to keep the fires going in winter and the candles lit on the Sabbath. The candles themselves were made of kosher wax."[25]

As the colonies became a nation, the most prominent Jewish religious personality of the generation was Gershom Mendes Seixas. Born in New York in 1745 to a Sephardic father and an Ashkenazic mother, Seixas served as hazzan of Shearith Israel, known today as the Spanish and Portuguese Synagogue, from 1768 to 1776 and again from 1784 to 1816. During the British occupation of New York, Seixas relocated to Philadelphia, where he functioned as minister of Mikveh Israel, 1780–84.[26]

Congregation Shearith Israel, at which Seixas received his education under the tutelage of Hazzan Pinto, maintained an all-day school from 1755 to 1776 and sporadically during the early decades of the nineteenth century.[27] Operation of such a school was designed to provide Hebrew and general education under Jewish auspices. It offered an alternative to education under non-Jewish, sectarian auspices.

In the early national period, nearly all schools in New York City, as elsewhere in the United States, were religious in character. Private "common pay" schools typically assumed the religious identity of their headmaster. "Free schools"—charity schools supported by churches—were eligible to secure state funding. Through a bequest, Shearith Israel created a charity school known as Polonies Talmud Torah. Beginning in 1811, the school benefited from state financial assistance parallel to funding received by Protestant and Catholic schools.[28] Shearith Israel joined with Presbyterian, Baptist, Methodist, and Catholic churches in strongly advocating state aid to church schools.[29] This lobbying effort was in response to challenges from the nondenominational New York Free School, forerunner of the Public School Society, which wanted all state money to flow into its institutions. Indeed, in New York, state support of religiously sponsored charity schools continued until 1825. Over the ensuing decades, throughout the country, public schools were gradually to achieve a monopoly over state funding of education.

For a number of years, Hazzan Seixas served as Shearith Israel's principal religious instructor. His contract of 1793 included the provision that he teach students "to read the Hebrew language and translate it into English."[30] It was further stipulated that "G. Seixas shall not exact any extra pay for a scholar who shall arrive to be Bar Mitzvah but shall be obliged to teach him everything requisite according to the capacity of such scholar."[31] It appears that education for the bar mitzvah ceremony at age thirteen, a significant focus of late-twentieth-century Jewish instruction in synagogue-sponsored religious schools, occupied a prominent place on the agenda of synagogue-based education in the early national period.

Rosters of the names of students enrolled indicate that girls as well as boys were among the school's students.[32] It is noteworthy that, in Western Europe, Samson Raphael Hirsch, in the middle of the nineteenth century, was the first Orthodox leader to advocate the systematic, school-based education of young girls. In Eastern Europe, girls' schooling was not systematically initiated in traditional circles until the early twentieth century. In the United States, the formal religious education of girls was already in evidence in the eighteenth century within congregations that, despite haphazard religious practice on the part of individual members, defined themselves in traditional terms. The celebration of the bar mitzvah—literally, "son of commandment"—milestone as part of the synagogue service remained exclusive to males. The celebration of bat mitzvah—"daughter of commandment"—as part of the synagogue service, an American innovation, was initiated only in the twentieth century.

Notwithstanding early-nineteenth-century state financial support for its school, Shearith Israel was unable to maintain a day school on a continuing basis. The reluctance of its members to enroll their children may have been a function of the lack of sustained educational leadership. When Emanuel N. Carvalho, a competent teacher who had come to New York from London, served as the school's headmaster from 1808 to 1811, there was a well-subscribed, full-day program; when Carvalho moved to Charleston, the school declined, experiencing years of intermittent openings and closings, apparently associated with the availability and ability of instructors.[33] A poignant call to congregants from three trustees early in the nineteenth century conveys the frustration of those endeavoring to maintain the school:

> In order to make your children truly virtuous you must rear them in the strict principles of our holy religion, and this cannot be efficiently done without their understanding what they are saying when addressing the deity.
>
> Education generally speaking is the first thing which ought to be pursued in life, in order to constitute us rational, how much then is to be expected from having in addition thereto, a complete and full knowledge of the Hebrew language being that in which all our prayers are read. Yet notwithstanding this, it is with regret that it is perceived few, very few indeed, are concerned about it.[34]

The focus of this plea on the importance of Hebrew language education for liturgical purposes manifests a curricular emphasis that was to recur frequently in American Jewish education.

Over time, it became the purpose of the Polonies Talmud Torah to provide religious instruction to children of the poor; as a charity school, it qualified—until 1825—for state aid as long as it provided general education as part of its program. The more affluent members of the community engaged private tutors.[35] In Charleston, home to the largest concentration of Jews in America in the early nineteenth century, the Jewish community made no provisions for a school—parents had to depend entirely on private tutors.[36] Similarly, it was not until 1853 that Savannah's Mickve Israel offered congregation-sponsored religious education.[37]

With a modest population, rapid acculturation, and virtually no educational infrastructure, Jewish learning in the early national period was negligible. In 1789, the Newport congregation reported that no one was able to read from the Torah and that the weekly Torah portion had to be read from a printed text.[38] One of the few learned Jews in the early national period, Manuel Josephson, stipulated in his will in 1796 that his Hebrew books, which included a library of rabbinic literature, be sent to his brother in Hamburg. It did not appear that there was or that there would be any call for such works in the United States.[39] The old guard of colonial days had, indeed, become deeply acculturated. Historian Arthur Hertzberg noted that "there is little doubt that before 1800 less than half of the grandchildren of the early Jewish settlers remained Jews."[40]

Rebecca Samuel, a young Jewish woman living in Petersburg, Virginia, in the 1790s, wrote a letter in Yiddish to her parents in Hamburg, describing her experience of Jewish life in the new nation:

> Dear parents, . . . Jewishness is pushed aside here. There are here [in Petersburg] ten or twelve Jews, and they are not worthy of being called Jews. We have a *shohet* [ritual slaughterer] here who goes to market and buys *terefah* [nonkosher] meat and then brings it home. On Rosh Ha-Shanah and on Yom Kippur the people worshiped here without one *sefer Torah* [Scroll of the Law], and not one of them wore the *tallit* [a large prayer shawl worn in the synagogue] or the *arba kanfot* [the small set of fringes worn on the body], except Hyman and my Sammy's godfather.

You can believe me that I crave to see a synagogue to which I can go. The way we live now is no life at all. We do not know what the Sabbath and the holidays are. On the Sabbath all the Jewish shops are open; and they do business on that day as they do throughout the whole week. But ours we do not allow to open. With us there is still some Sabbath. You must believe me that in our house we all live as Jews as much as we can.[41]

Reflecting the reality that Jewish education was a home-based, parental responsibility, Rebecca noted that she had taught her three-year-old daughter bedtime prayers and the grace after meals. To satisfy her family's religious needs, Rebecca looked forward to moving to Charleston, with its larger Jewish community. In the same letter, she observed that the United States was a land of tremendous economic opportunity and that the non-Jewish population was most accepting.[42] America was, for Rebecca Samuel—as it was later for many other Jews—a mixed blessing.

With escalating immigration of Jews from German-speaking lands from 1820 to 1840, a dozen new synagogues were established, bringing the total of formally organized Jewish congregations in the United States to eighteen by 1840.[43] In each case, congregants established and governed their synagogue affairs with autonomous determination as to ritual and organizational procedures. Efforts were made, at least in the public arena, to emulate the practices of the Old Country. One significant outgrowth of immigration was a gradual broadening of responsibility for Jewish education, beyond the family.

Emergence of Sunday Schools

As public schools became preeminent, many Christian Sunday schools, initially established by benevolent societies to provide poor children with general, as well as Christian religious, educational opportunity, came to focus exclusively on religious instruction. By 1838, there were 8,000 such Christian schools in the United States.[44] Women played a leading role in this development.

America's growing, increasingly literate, population created an expanded market for printed material. Women's magazines and novels of the 1820s and 1830s helped to promote contemporary women's culture.

Among the values that such literature supported was the mission of women in the religious education of children. Acknowledging the inspiration of the Christian Sunday school movement, American-born Rebecca Gratz, a member of a prominent Jewish family of merchants and community leaders in Philadelphia, launched the Hebrew Sunday School Society in 1838. Gratz, who had earlier aided in founding the Female Hebrew Benevolent Society (FHBS), noted: "[W]e have never yet had a Sunday school in our congregation and so I have induced our ladies to follow the example of other religious communities."[45] The school that Rebecca Gratz envisioned would enable Jewish boys and girls—including the growing immigrant population—to face and refute evangelists who aimed to convert Jews to Christianity.

One month after Rebecca Gratz secured approval of the FHBS for her educational project, her Hebrew Sunday school opened with fifty students and six teachers, including Gratz, who served as superintendent. The all-female, volunteer faculty was composed of women respected for their intelligence and moral character. From the outset, the Jewish Sunday school movement was, like its Protestant counterpart, a women's movement. Starting with the Philadelphia prototype, women founded, directed, and taught at the schools, which were attended by girls as well as boys. Because the religious education of children was considered part of the domain of women in America, it was axiomatic that women required religious education to properly educate their children.[46] Gratz's most recent biographer, Dianne Ashton, observes that the bibliocentric, creedal curriculum of the school reflected the fact that none of the school's founders possessed substantial Jewish learning.[47] Fiscal support for the Sunday school came from the FHBS, private donors, and Mikveh Israel, Philadelphia's well-established Sephardic congregation. Additionally, an annual appeal was held at a festive public examination, and parents who had the means to do so paid $2 per year.[48]

Gratz's efforts benefited from the support of the hazzan of Mikveh Israel, Isaac Leeser. Leeser had emigrated from Westphalia to Richmond, Virginia, in 1824, at the age of eighteen. His formal Jewish education ended during his adolescence, and he attended the gymnasium of Münster for two and a quarter years prior to his emigration. Leeser's uncle in Richmond had married a relative of the Seixas family, and this connection served as an entrée for Leeser to the better-established Jews in the community. Leeser assisted the hazzan at Richmond's Sephardic congregation, Beth Shalome, and worked to achieve mastery of the Eng-

lish language. By 1828, he was able to publish two articles in the Richmond *Whig* responding to a defamatory article against Jews and Judaism. In 1829, this twenty-three-year-old German Jewish immigrant
was elected hazzan—chief religious functionary—of Philadelphia's
Sephardic congregation Mikveh Israel, testimony to Leeser's ability as
well as to the paucity of well-trained candidates for such positions.[49] So
far-reaching was Leeser's impact on American Jewish life in the decades
ahead—through his books, Bible translation, and monthly journal—that
1830–60 has been dubbed the "Age of Leeser."[50]

In 1838, Leeser published *The Hebrew Reader* for students. Soon
after the opening of the Sunday school, in 1839, he authored *Catechism
for Younger Children*. Commenting on the Sunday school phenomenon,
Leeser observed:

> [S]ome prejudice was at first manifested by various persons,
> who fancied that they discovered an objectionable imitation of
> gentile practices in this undertaking, forgetting that it is the first
> duty of Israel to instill knowledge of divine things in the hearts
> of the young, and this institution was eminently calculated to
> bestow this necessary blessing alike upon rich and poor without
> fee or price. It is but seldom that so noble an aim has been
> sought after, begun solely for the glorification of our Maker and
> the well-being of his people; it is therefore gratifying to record,
> that this unfounded prejudice has nearly died away, and one
> cannot give a better evidence of the fact, than that now fully
> one hundred children are enrolled, and what is more, that
> nearly all attend whenever the weather is at all favorable, and
> this despite the great distance which many of the scholars and
> teachers have to walk, living as they do in almost every part of
> the city and suburbs.[51]

Leeser noted approvingly that "the example set in this city was followed
in New York and Charleston about the same time; and there, as well as
here, the superintendence and teaching are in the hands of the ladies."[52]

The ambience, values, and program of the Sunday school are recol-
lected by Rosa Mordecai, great-niece of Rebecca Gratz and a student at
her great-aunt's Sunday school:

> The room in which we assembled was a large one with four
> long windows at the end. Between the centre windows was a

raised platform with a smaller one upon which stood a table and a chair. On the table was a much worn Bible containing both the Old and the New Testaments (Rev. Isaac Leeser's valuable edition of the Hebrew Bible had not then been published), a hand-bell, Watts' Hymns, and a penny contribution box "for the poor of Jerusalem."

Here Miss Gratz presided. A stately, commanding figure, always neatly dressed in plain black, with thin white collar and cuffs, close-fitting bonnet over her curled front, which time never touched with grey, giving her, even in her most advanced years, a youthful appearance. Her eyes would pierce every part of the hall and often detect mischief which escaped the notice of the teachers.

The only punishment, I can recall, was for the delinquent to be marched through the school and seated upon the little platform, before mentioned, under the table. Sometimes this stand would be quite full, and I was rather disposed to envy those children who had no lessons to say. But, her duties over, Miss Gratz would call them by name to stand before her for reproof, which, apparently mild, was so soul-stirring that even the most hardened sinner would quail before it. She was extremely particular to instill neatness and cleanliness. A soiled dress, crooked collar, or sticky hands never escaped her penetrating glance and the reproof or remedy was instantaneous.

Many old scholars can still recall the question: "Who formed you child and made you live?" and the answer: "God did my life and spirit give"—the first lines of that admirable "Pyke's Catechism," which long held its place in the Sunday School, and was, I believe, the first book printed for it. The "Scripture Lessons" were taught from a little illustrated work published by the Christian Sunday School Union. Many a long summer's day have I spent, pasting pieces of paper over answers unsuitable for Jewish children, and many were the fruitless efforts of those children to read through, or under the hidden lines.[53]

As is evident from Rosa Mordecai's description, Jewish Sunday schools reinforced the middle-class values of public schools and Protestant Sunday schools: order, punctuality, obedience, self-discipline, and cleanliness. Jewish Sunday schools embraced the Protestant division between universal morality—the domain of public education—and particularistic

forms that were appropriately the sphere of supplementary religious education. Given the school's raison d'être, it was essential that uniquely
Jewish materials be developed for religious instruction. While the Sunday school movement served, in part, to Americanize Jewish children,
the founders of the Philadelphia Hebrew Sunday School viewed themselves as Jewish traditionalists and were opposed to religious reform.[54]
Reflecting the religious ethos of the era, the scope of knowledge of its
faculty, and the agenda of protecting students from evangelical efforts,
the Philadelphia school's curriculum focused on the unity of God, stories from the Hebrew Bible (in English translation), and the Ten Com-
mandments.

Although, as Leeser intimated, some German Jewish congregations
considered Sunday schools a "distasteful imitation of Protestantism," by
1845, Jewish Sunday schools had been established in several other communities, including Cincinnati and Richmond.[55] In Richmond, it was
the ladies' auxiliary of Beth Shalome that initiated a Sunday school. The
school was sustained by a series of annual balls, open to and supported
by the entire community. As the Richmond *Daily Enquirer* reported:
"[T]he Hebrew School Fund Ball was a brilliant affair, and we trust that
much good may result from it."[56] Like the Philadelphia model, Saturday
and Sunday schools established in other locales were conducted on a coeducational basis.[57]

In the preface to his *Catechism for Younger Children,* Leeser ac-
knowledged his indebtedness to a work by Eduard Kley of Hamburg titled *Catechismus der mosaischen Religion,* which appeared in 1814.
Notwithstanding the fact that Leeser championed Jewish traditionalism
in practice throughout his career and that Kley was among the founders
of the Hamburg Reform Temple, Leeser affirmed: "I would not detract
the least from the merits of this learned and eloquent man despite of his
errors; and I gladly admit that my labour was much abridged, by having
so excellent a guide as he has furnished."[58] The style and content of the
book can be gleaned from its opening lines:

Q: What is religion?
A: Religion is the knowledge we have of God, and the duties
    we owe in obedience to His will.
Q: What do you mean by saying, "I believe in God"?
A: I believe that everything I see around me, the trees, the
    flowers, the earth, the water, also the sun and the moon,
    and the thousands of bright stars that shine so beautifully

in the sky, were made by the "great Creator" whom we call "The Almighty God."[59]

The catechism moves from religion in general to the "Mosaic religion," affirming the divine origin of the Torah and its proper interpretation by the sages. Inasmuch as the Torah is divinely revealed and rabbinic interpretation of its instructions is correct, for Leeser it followed that both the moral and ceremonial laws are imperative. The catechism concludes with Maimonides' Thirteen Principles of Faith. Leeser's *Hebrew Reader: Designed as an Easy Guide to the Hebrew Tongue, for Jewish Children and Self-Instruction* devotes twenty-three pages to the development of skills for Hebrew reading, with the ensuing twenty-five pages—consistent with the previously noted emphasis on developing the skills necessary to participate in the synagogue prayer service—applying those lessons to such recurring prayers as *Adon olam, Shema, Ma tovu, Modeh ani,* the opening paragraph of *Birkat ha-mazon,* and *Yigdal.*[60] The work was reprinted a number of times, but Leeser lamented, in his preface to the fourth edition in 1856, that though the book "has met with approbation, still the sale has been very slow, the demand for the various schools being quite small."[61] Rebecca Gratz's Sunday school did not include Hebrew in its curriculum.

Leeser, who founded a short-lived Jewish publication society in 1845, produced dozens of printed works, along with a widely disseminated periodical. Improvements in print technology and the declining cost of printed material led, at mid-century, to expanded publications of all kinds, including evangelical literature. Consequently, Jewish education and Jewish educational materials were essential both to strengthen the faith and to protect against missionaries proselytizing among Jews.[62] It was Isaac Leeser who produced the first English translation of the Bible starting with the Pentateuch, in 1845, and proceeding to the complete text of the Bible, in 1853.

The Case for Jewish Day Schools

Even as he expressed high regard for the work of Rebecca Gratz and her assistants, Leeser urged the establishment of an all-day Jewish school for two reasons. First, it was impossible to achieve Hebrew literacy in "extra" hours, and "I tell you, without in the least qualifying my assertion, that without an adequate knowledge of the Hebrew, sufficient at least to understand the Scriptures and the ordinary prayers, no Jew can allege that he has acquired that knowledge which is all in all to him. A Hebrew not to be a Hebrew in language when this is within his reach, is an absurd proposition which requires no argument to illustrate."[63] Second, the public or private schools were, in Leeser's view, essentially Christian. "[W]e are in great error if we suppose that Christian teachers do not endeavor to influence actively the sentiments of their Jewish pupils."[64] Moreover, "I deem it even of doubtful expediency to have the reading of the Bible, out of what many call (non) sectarian version, enforced, though the book used should be without note or comment; for, as soon as a particular Bible-version is chosen, the favoured society using this translation in their churches have the advantage over all others who reject it."[65] It was the Protestant tenor of public education to which Leeser pointed that led Catholics to establish an extensive network of parochial schools.

As for the concern that a Jewish day school might divert time from general education, thereby diminishing from students' educational attainments, Leeser commented:

> We will admit for argument's sake, that by this (religious) study the hours to be devoted to grammar, history and other sciences should have to be diminished: still can this be called a loss. For let us ask, what do you want to teach by sciences? Certainly nothing more, than to give to the young correct views of life, and enable them to judge with propriety of things to be hereafter presented to them. So is grammar, to enable them to speak and write with propriety; history, to inform them of the acts of past ages, and to give them examples of good men to be imitated and wicked ones whose deeds should be abhorred; and so with other things. Now we demand, Is religious knowledge not something which is to become useful to children hereafter? Is it not calculated to enable them to judge with propriety of many subjects of the highest importance? If you then call sciences the ornament of life, religion surely is far more, it is the essential element of our existence; and hence it is a science above all to be acquired with diligent study.[66]

Jewish studies thus represented an enhancement of students' education, adding to and deepening each dimension of study and providing essential grounding for leading a meaningful Jewish life. Where it was impracticable to conduct day schools, Leeser counseled that supplementary education be strengthened; hence, his support of Rebecca Gratz's Sunday school initiative. He advised that parents keep close watch and "not suffer on any account, that the young Israelites should be instructed in matters of religion belonging to another creed."[67]

Leeser observed that "few indeed can be found who give not some schooling to their children, and many spend large and liberal sums to teach them whatever is instrumental and useful. . . . [Y]et these very parents find it impossible to pay for the religious education of their children."[68] In their rush to get ahead in American life, too many parents, chided Leeser, neglected Jewish education.

As to the agenda of launching day schools, Leeser recognized that the wealthy "exclusives" would not be the first to send their children to such schools—preferring, rather, to mingle with better classes of Christian society—but "let them only see that [the Jewish day schools] are well conducted; that order and decorum reign among those who frequent them; that there are those in attendance whose friendship and acquaintance will be a source of comfort to their fellow scholars in after [post-school]-life: and our word for it, they will soon learn to forgo their silly prejudices."[69] Leeser wrote at a time when public schools had not yet become ubiquitous and when for many families education was, in any case, private. His recognition of the need to market day schools as centers of excellence in education with value-added community and spiritual dimensions was to be echoed in the late twentieth century as day school advocates actively sought to broaden the base of attendees.

By 1840, the first stirrings of a broader, communal responsibility— extending beyond the family—for the provision of Jewish education were in evidence. Mechanical reading of Hebrew, primarily for relating to the synagogue service, continued to be a significant educational goal. Instruction in the tenets of the faith was conducted through recitation of catechisms, a common pedagogic vehicle of the day. As reflected in the course of study and supplementary frameworks—tutorial or a very limited-time, school-based instruction—of Jewish learning, Jewish education was designed to nurture a sense of connection and belonging as well as the ability to participate in public prayers and religious ceremonies among students. For males, preparation for a synagogue bar mitzvah ceremony was an integral part of religious instruction. Jewish education explicitly and implicitly affirmed a spirit of universalism; in that spirit, biblical texts rather than rabbinic literature were the principal classical works explored.

While Jews had experienced population growth from 2,000 to 15,000 from 1776 to 1840, the ensuing generation brought the first mass migration of Jews to the new nation. In the decades preceding the Civil War, scores of new synagogues and Jewish schools were to be established, as more Jews settled in the United States and, in many cases, moved west. With this growth in population came expanded Jewish educational initiatives.

CHAPTER TWO
Educational Currents in an Era of Heightened Immigration, 1840–80

From 1840 to 1880, the American Jewish community grew from 15,000 to 250,000, resulting primarily from the immigration of Jews from German-speaking lands. The massive wave of Eastern European immigration began after 1880, but by 1880 one-sixth of America's Jews had been born in lands east of Germany.[70] New social welfare and Jewish cultural institutions were established by the immigrants, including new frameworks of Jewish education. Although some of these institutions, such as Jewish day schools, were not to survive the immigrant generation, others, such as the Hebrew Union College and Young Men's Hebrew Associations—precursors of Jewish Community Centers—were to flourish and endure.

Between 1840 and 1860, 4.2 million European immigrants landed in the United States. German immigrants were a close second to Irish newcomers to the U.S. in these decades.[71] Jews, like Protestants and Catholics from the various German kingdoms and principalities, maintained a strong affinity for their German language and heritage, even as they adapted to American life.

Immigrant Jews spread throughout the country; in 1850, 70 percent of the Jews in the United States were peddlers.[72] As a consequence of population growth and geographic diffusion, the number of congregations grew from eighteen to 277 by 1877. In addition to establishing new congregations, German Jewish immigrants created a broad range of social, cultural, and charitable organizations. One of the earliest of these organizations was B'nai B'rith, established in 1843. Like other such American associations, it was composed of local lodges, coordinated by district and national bodies. As in the first-generation German Jewish synagogues in America, German was the language of most lodges in the early decades. B'nai B'rith offered its members typical lodge benefits, giving loans to the needy, assisting the sick, burying the dead, and aiding widows and orphans. Like other Americans, German Jewish immigrants and their American-born children established myriad social welfare agencies. Although synagogues still engaged in charity, by the mid-nineteenth century other social service organizations had supplanted them in the arena of charitable activity. The growth of these institutions left synagogues as custodians of a narrowed sphere of religious matters, including Jewish education.[73]

A Generation of German Jewish
Day Schools in America

In 1847, Bohemian-born Isaac Mayer Wise, who had arrived in the United States but one year earlier and was serving as rabbi of Beth El Congregation in Albany, New York, wrote a letter to the Leipzig *Allgemeine Zeitung des Judenthums,* in which he described the rapid growth of Jewish communities throughout the United States:

> New congregations are arising everywhere in the United States: in Rochester and Buffalo, in the State of New York; in Bangor, Maine; in Hartford, Connecticut; Newark and Paterson, New Jersey; Chicago, Illinois; and in Montgomery, Alabama, new German-Jewish congregations have recently formed. To be sure, they all begin by merely furnishing a room for worship, buying a *Sefer Torah* [Torah scroll], and appointing a Hazzan, since at the beginning such a congregation usually consists of a mere 20 to 40 members.
>
> But if one returns to such a congregation after two or three years, one is sure to find a fine building on an elegant street, bearing the inscription: Synagogue for the Children of Israel.[74]

In the realm of Jewish education, Wise's observations were not as effusive. After noting that in most communities there was no Jewish school of any kind, he described three types of schools, one type of which he felt held great promise:

> In a few [communities] the Hazzan teaches Hebrew reading and has the children read a little in various catechisms, and fre-

quently the miracle occurs that a boy learns to render the *Negi-nah* [chant] and a few chapters of *Chumash* [Pentateuch] into German.

In other congregations they have introduced a phantom affair called a Sunday School. There religious instruction for children is imparted each Sabbath or Sunday by good-hearted young women. What fruits these few hours can bring forth hardly necessitates further description.

I am greatly pleased to be able to draw your attention to a young vigorously flourishing "Hebrew-English Institution" in New York, and to others in Albany, New Orleans and Cincinnati where Hebrew, English and German instruction is carried on zealously and with the best results by qualified teachers.[75]

Wise, like Leeser, saw the time on task available for Jewish learning in supplementary settings as inadequate and was critical of both the curriculum and qualifications of those who taught in supplementary Jewish schools to deliver substantial or even adequate Jewish education.

Though they were to be antagonists in the ensuing debate between traditionalists and religious reformers, Wise and Leeser were in agreement in the late 1840s about the inherent impossibility of satisfactory Jewish schooling in a Sunday school context. Shortly before Wise dispatched his assessment, Leeser wrote in *The Occident*, his monthly journal:

On one day of the week, in some congregations, the ladies give instruction in Catechism, in Bible Questions, and Scriptural Recitations, to such as are willing to come; they have no means of compelling a regular attendance, and several of the teachers have generally to be absent also, from some cause or other. Unfavourable weather, also, not rarely interrupts the exercises, and if holydays beside intervene, there may be several weeks consecutively that no instruction can be imparted. And then, above all, though it is so desirable that the Hebrew language shall be taught, there is no time to teach it, should there be even a sufficient number of competent instructors within reach; the two or three hours every week are barely enough to impart the elementary rudiments of the principles of religion, without which knowledge not the smallest child should be suffered to remain; and how then shall the Hebrew be taught at the same time?[76]

Not only were a few hours a week insufficient time in which to achieve Jewish educational goals but, as Leeser observed, absence from school—of student or teacher—further diminished from the already scant available sessions. Competent instructors were in short supply, and the possibility of acquiring Hebrew knowledge in a limited, part-time framework was nil. A contributor to *The Occident* in Boston in 1844, reflecting the inadequacy of Jewish education as well as the prevalence of bar mitzvah ceremonies, suggested that rather than celebrating the occasion of bar mitzvah as a mere function of chronological age, a demonstration of knowledge of the "precepts of the divine law" on the part of the thirteen-year-old would be desirable.[77]

Mid-nineteenth-century Jewish educational realities are conveyed by the son of Rabbi Bernard Illowy, a champion of Jewish traditionalism in the United States in the 1850s and 1860s. Illowy, a Bohemian-born, European-trained Orthodox rabbi, arrived in the United States in 1853, and served as rabbi in a number of communities, including Philadelphia, Syracuse, Baltimore, Cincinnati, St. Louis, and New Orleans. Of his father's American rabbinic career, Dr. Henry Illoway (who added an "a" to the family name) relates that he

> . . . always held it as a matter of first importance that the children of his congregants should be taught Hebrew, the Bible, and the tenets of their faith, and where no schools existed, he established them, as in Syracuse, in Baltimore, in New Orleans, in Cincinnati. In these institutions all the branches of instruction of the public schools were taught by a full corps of competent teachers besides having Hebrew, the Bible, and the principles of the faith (Leeser's *Catechism* was the text-book chiefly used for this) in the curriculum.
>
> For the same reason, and because in this way children could be reached, who for one reason or another did not attend the congregational (day) school, he introduced the confirmation on Shabuot. . . . Six months before Shabuot the class began its work, instruction in Bible history, in the tenets of the faith and its ceremonials, in the ceremonial laws and in the prayers. Boys who had not learned to lay *Tephillin* (phylacteries) were taught to do so and were impressed with the necessity of doing so every morning.[78]

Illowy, an Orthodox rabbi who corresponded with European halakhic authorities and published learned responsa, adopted the confirmation ceremony that had been introduced by religious reformers. Consistent with the American pattern of equal educational opportunity for children of both sexes, it appears that the only gender-based curricular difference in the training he provided was in the matter of teaching boys to don tefillin.

Leeser's vision of all-day Jewish schools in the United States was realized in the 1840s, as German Jewish immigrants, arriving at a time before public schools had achieved preeminence, and desiring to maintain both their German and Jewish heritage, created more than two dozen such schools. By the 1850s, seven Jewish day schools had been established in New York, enrolling more than a thousand students.[79] Similar schools were launched in Philadelphia, Baltimore, Chicago, Boston, Albany, Cincinnati, Detroit, Essex County (New Jersey), Pittsburgh, and Washington, D.C.[80] Typical of these schools was the one organized by Kehilath Anshe Ma'ariv Congregation in Chicago in 1853. The school was modeled after such schools in Germany, where the curriculum included general studies augmented by instruction in Jewish religion, Hebrew prayers, and Bible reading in German translation. In addition to English, German, arithmetic, geography, drawing, and singing, the K.A.M. curriculum featured prayers and readings from the Pentateuch, as well as catechism relating to Jewish religion and history. The common school branches were taught by non-Jewish instructors, and a rabbi or cantor was responsible for Jewish studies.[81] The dedication of German Jewish immigrants to maintaining German culture is manifested in the fact that of the seventeen mid-nineteenth-century Jewish day schools with extant curricular information, all schools included German.[82]

A number of private boarding schools teaching Jewish as well as secular subjects operated in the middle of the nineteenth century.[83] The creation of a variety of day schools by this generation of German Jewish immigrants reflected several interests, including, in addition to the provision of Jewish education, preservation of German culture, a desire for quality assurance in education—inasmuch as the developing public schools were not always perceived as outstanding—and concern about religious sectarianism in public schools. Mid-nineteenth-century Jewish day schools were coeducational, with female students constituting one-third of the schools' enrollment.[84]

The intensive Hebrew education envisioned by Leeser as a cornerstone of day school possibility was by no means of paramount interest in all such schools. An alumna of an 1860s Cincinnati day school recalled: "A schoolhouse was in the annex of the synagogue which most all of the children of the members of the congregation attended. We were taught English and Hebrew. The *Chumish* I could not understand, and told my beloved father I could not see why it was taught us [in Hebrew] and please to have the teachers do away with it. As he was president of the congregation then, he brought it before the board, who quite agreed with me, and I was very happy after it was removed from our studies."[85] The debate over educating for Hebrew proficiency versus Jewish study in translation was to be a recurring theme in considerations of school-based curriculum and instruction in ensuing generations.

In the 1840s, Hebrew literary associations, conducting lectures and maintaining libraries, were established by young German Jewish immigrants in several cities. Based on Jewish newspaper references, it would appear that literary discussion groups were most typically conducted separately by and for men and women.[86] As an outgrowth of such literary associations, a new type of organization, the Young Men's Hebrew Association (YMHA), was initiated in a number of communities. The first YMHA had been founded in Baltimore in 1854, but had suspended its activities between 1860 and 1868 because of the Civil War and its aftermath. YMHAs aimed to promote knowledge of the history, literature, and doctrines of Judaism. The "Y" often included a library of Jewish reading material and offered classes and lectures in Jewish history and Hebrew language for young men and women.[87] YMHAs provided a congenial social and intellectual milieu for Jewish young adults; by 1890, more than 120 YMHA branches had been established.[88]

Those Jews who had, by mid-century, become economically secure recognized the importance of Jewish education as a means of protecting immigrant youth, particularly those living in poor neighborhoods, from missionary activity directed at them. On New York's Lower East Side, Christian missionaries conducted a school teaching Jewish children Bible in Hebrew. As a countermeasure, Hebrew Free Schools were organized in the 1860s by the joint efforts of several New York congregations. In like manner, Jewish YMHAs introduced gymnasia and sports in imitation of YMCAs, to counter missionary influence.

In the development of American Jewry, the decades from 1840 to 1880 were primarily a period of Western and Central European Jewish settlement and institution building, but a stream of immigration from Eastern Europe was already quite apparent by the 1850s.[89] The first Eastern European congregation founded in New York, Beth Hamedrash Hagodol, was established in 1852. In 1857, Pesach Rosenthal, a peddler who had been a teacher in the Old Country, opened a Talmud Torah—

supplementary Jewish school—in his home on the East Side to provide Jewish education to children after public school hours. This school, in which the language of instruction was Yiddish, was to metamorphose into the Machzikei—"those who support"—Talmud Torah, one of the better-organized communal supplementary schools in the 1880s.[90]

As public schools became the exclusive beneficiaries of state funding, their facilities and faculty came to be viewed as highly desirable for accessing the best education. Jews, unlike Catholics, increasingly opted for public schooling. An example of the prevailing situation was the rise and fall of the St. Louis Hebrew Day School between November 1854 and February 1855. The school was founded at the initiative of Rabbi Illowy, who had recently arrived in the community as its first rabbi. Though initially agreeing to the rabbi's day school project, the board soon opted to change the school to a Sunday school. Isidor Bush, an active member of the board, opined that public schools could provide better general education and that the limited available Jewish resources could be more effectively used to offer quality Sunday and evening instruction.[91] By the 1870s, public school education had become a given for American-born Jewish parents with children of school age. As acculturated Americans, they did not possess their parents' zeal for the preservation of valued "old world" culture. Moreover, public schools had earned recognition for providing quality educational opportunity. By 1875, no Jewish day schools remained in operation anywhere in the United States.

Although Sunday schools had proliferated by the 1860s, the lack of well-qualified teachers—most instructors were young volunteers—combined with the acculturation and diminishing interest of many second-generation families, gave rise to growing concern about the efficacy of these schools as vehicles of religious instruction. This malaise was conveyed in 1880 by Professor B. A. Abrams, assistant superintendent of schools in Milwaukee:

> Let's admit it openly: how many of the teachers who assist our preachers with the administration of the religious schools deserve, in reality, the name teacher? How many of them possess, besides some smattering of the Hebrew language, the abilities which would enable them to be in charge of a religious education of those entrusted to their care? The logical result is lack of respect for the teacher and an aversion against instruction and the school.

> But even the activity of the best teacher cannot be fruitful if he has to fight against the indifference in the home. It is a strange fact that parents who take great care to see to it that their children attend public school regularly and punctually keep the very same children at home for nonsensical reasons, since it is only Sabbath School that they are missing. A mere whim of the child, a party, a music lesson, are often considered important enough to justify an absence from religious school.[92]

Not only were qualified instructional personnel in short supply; parental support of religious schooling for their children—even among those who were enrolled—reflected considerable ambivalence about the importance of Jewish education.

Acculturation and Reform

German-speaking Jewish immigrants of the mid-nineteenth century were, by and large, of traditional Jewish background. The absence of rabbinic leadership or a well-developed religious communal structure, the quest for economic and social advancement, and the local milieu affected the course of Jewish religious practice. Though not irreligious, immigrants set their own standards of Jewish practice. Abraham Rice, a staunch traditionalist, was the first ordained rabbi to settle in the United States, arriving in 1840. To his former teacher Wolf Hamburger, Rabbi Rice wrote in 1849: "The character of religious life in this land is on the lowest level; most of the people are eating nonkosher food, are violating the Shabbos in public . . . and there are thousands who have been assimilated among the non-Jewish population."[93] Notwithstanding Rice's critique, the exponential growth in the number of synagogues, the hiring of *shohtim* (ritual slaughterers), and the establishment of Jewish schools attest to the desire among many of the immigrant generation to identify as Jews and to transmit this identity to their children.

Rice's experiences as a rabbi in the United States were frustrating. Early in his rabbinate at Baltimore Hebrew Congregation, Rice attempted to enforce a bylaw that prohibited Sabbath violators from being called to the Torah. Upon being advised by the trustees that the rule could not be enforced, Rice asked that, when such offenders were called to the Torah, congregants desist from responding "amen" to their blessings. Such was the very limited extent of rabbinical authority in the United States.[94]

Although many immigrant German-speaking Jews were lax in their Jewish ritual practices, it was only in the latter half of the nineteenth century that Reform Judaism took root in the United States. The first stirrings of reform were expressed in 1824, when forty-seven members of Beth Elohim in Charleston petitioned for changes in the Orthodox ritual. The petition asked that a weekly sermon be instituted, that the service be abridged, and that a portion of the prayers be recited in English. Rebuffed by congregational authorities, a number of the petitioners organized "The Reformed Society of Israelites." Although the society disbanded in 1833, Beth Elohim itself installed an organ in 1840, and, in 1841, its more traditional members seceded and formed a new congregation, Shearith Israel.[95]

Historian Michael Meyer attributes the rise of the Reform movement at mid-century to Germanizing as well as Americanizing trends. The first generation of Jewish immigrants from German-speaking lands was, in the main, from small towns and villages; they came in search of economic betterment. Meyer observes that though poorly educated, they were traditionalists in their public ritual, if not in personal practice. In the 1840s and 1850s, more affluent, better-educated Jews made their way to the United States. Among the newcomers were some who had become acquainted with and embraced the movement for reform. This wave of immigrants encountered earlier settlers who saw in reform a means of religious Americanization. The German Jewish Reform leaders who came at mid-century tapped into a wellspring of readiness for an articulated vision of Reform Judaism.[96]

David Einhorn, a leading Reform activist who had participated in the Reform rabbinical conferences at Frankfurt and Breslau in 1845 and 1846, relocated to the United States in 1855 to assume a pulpit at the invitation of an American Reform group.[97] Both before and during the German conferences, Einhorn had urged a vision of messianic redemption as against a redeemer and advocated German, as opposed to Hebrew, as the preferred language of religious expression. Hebrew, after all, represented Jewish nationality, which no longer existed; German was the language with which German Jews could best express their spiritual, religious consciousness and aspirations.

In his inaugural sermon at the Har Sinai Verein in Baltimore, Einhorn included a message on Jewish education emerging from the Reform outlook:

Shall we imbue our youth, free among free men, with a Judaism that would perpetuate the barriers between Israel and other peoples, isolate the Jew from the rest of mankind, and oppose with its hopes and aims the mighty current of modern life? Shall we attempt to bring them to synagogues where mediaeval laments resound, where prayers are intoned for our return to our ancient land, for the restoration of the sacrificial cult, and for the erection of Israel into a kingdom? Do this, and we shall have only indifference and contempt, if not positive hatred, for that for which we have sought to win their love. There is only one way to reach our high aim and that we will follow. We will point out to our children the world-redeeming power, the ever widening significance of the Sinaitic teaching which is ever enduring; the changeable character of its outward forms; the glorious triumphs it has achieved outside of the house of Jacob; the unparalleled sacrifices its preservation has cost; the wonderful vitality with which it has marched on, unscathed, amid the crash of worlds. . . . [A]nd, finally, the mission of our scattered people to carry the Law of God to all peoples and all climes.[98]

This emphasis on the universal and rejection of Jewish nationality, as reflected in a vision of the restoration of Israel and denunciation of ceremonialism, expressed the ideological position that was to be spelled out in the Reform Pittsburgh Platform of 1885, authored by Einhorn's son-in-law, Kaufmann Kohler.

It was, however, Isaac Mayer Wise who was the master institution builder of Reform Judaism in the United States. Following the model of Isaac Leeser, who had in 1843 established the monthly journal *The Occident* as a platform to express his traditionalist religious views and educational agenda, Isaac Mayer Wise launched an English-language weekly called *The Israelite* in 1854 as a platform for reform.[99] While of divergent views, both Leeser and Wise called for some form of union among the growing number of American congregations and urged the creation of a school of higher Jewish learning on American soil for the training of rabbis. With 150,000 Jews living in the United States by 1860, it was clear to traditionalists and reformers that the sustained vitality—as Jews—of American Jewry required indigenous religious leadership.

Efforts at union were undertaken in the 1850s and 1860s, including the creation in 1859 of a national Jewish defense organization, the

Board of Delegates of American Israelites, modeled after the Board of Deputies of British Jewry.[100] In 1867, the Board of Delegates of American Israelites and the Hebrew Education Society of Philadelphia—acting largely at the urging of Isaac Leeser—opened Maimonides College in Philadelphia. The school was launched with three students and did not grow over time; it finally closed its doors in 1873. In 1868, Temple Emanu-El of New York opened a theological seminary that operated with limited enrollment for a few years.[101]

In 1873, Isaac Mayer Wise was successful in organizing the Union of American Hebrew Congregations (UAHC), with thirty-four participating synagogues. At first, only midwestern and southern congregations affiliated with the union, but eastern seaboard congregations joined within a few years. The union, in 1875, sponsored the establishment of the Hebrew Union College (HUC) for the preparation of rabbis for the expanding American Jewish community. The college, based in Cincinnati, with Isaac Mayer Wise as its president, was to grow and endure. Though Wise had once imagined the possibility of a "Minhag America"—an "American Way"—among the Jews of the United States (indeed, he published a prayer book of that title in 1857), the UAHC and the HUC were destined to become primary institutional frameworks of American Reform Judaism. The beleaguered state of traditionalism by the 1860s can be sensed from the remarks, however exaggerated they may have been, of Rabbi Bernard Illowy. In 1862, he lamented: "[W]e must acknowledge to our own shame, because it is an undeniable fact, that since the downfall of the Jewish monarchy there has been no age and no country in which the Israelites were more denigrated and more indifferent toward their religion than in our age and in our country. . . . Yes, run through the streets of all our large congregations, and seek . . . whether you can find ten men . . . who still adhere faithfully to the faith of our fathers."[102]

Wise's vision of the Cincinnati rabbinical school that he successfully launched was significantly informed by the model of modern, nineteenth-century European rabbinical seminaries. Wise defined the curriculum of the college as "the Bible, with its Commentaries and Paraphrases, the Talmud and its Commentaries, the Jewish philosophical literature, all in their respective original tongues, the Theology, Ethics and History of the Hebrews, together with the various disciplines of Hermeneutics, Exegetics, Homiletics, Criticism and Semitic philology."[103] The program included contemporary academic categories, as well as classical texts, to be studied "scientifically." Initially, the college included teenage boys in a four-year preparatory department within which students not only undertook Jewish study at HUC but also earned a baccalaureate degree at a university. The first group of ordinands did not complete the rabbinical program until 1883.

Embracing the Public School

The ideal of public school education had become prominent in the Jacksonian 1830s. While democratic thinkers looked to the spread of knowledge as a basis for equalizing the distribution of power, people of means and a more conservative outlook saw public education as a measure against social disintegration—particularly at a time of escalating immigration. As public, nonsectarian education became prevalent, and was perceived as superior in resources and academic excellence to what was available in the fledgling Jewish day schools, the full-day Jewish schools closed, one by one, often becoming Sunday schools.[104] Then, as they did subsequently, Jewish parents sent their children to schools that they felt would best develop their skills and ability to live in American society. Describing Jewish educational institutions in Cincinnati to the United States Commissioner of Education in 1870, Isaac Mayer Wise— at one time a proponent of day schools—summed up the perspective of most American Jews: "It is our settled opinion here that the education of the young is the business of the State, and the religious instruction, to which we add the Hebrew, is the duty of religious bodies. Neither ought to interfere with the other. The secular branches belong to the public schools, religion in the Sabbath schools, exclusively."[105] Rather than public education as merely a pragmatic option, given a level of financing that might more effectively deliver general education, Wise expressed the prevailing view among American Jews that the public school was the proper locus of general education as a matter of principle. American Jews were at home in the United States, and the proper place for religious instruction seemed to be the family home and synagogue.

While sharing with Wise a deep commitment to religious reform, Rabbi Bernard Felsenthal of Chicago urged a different course in the sphere of Jewish learning:

We would be entirely against specifically Jewish schools, if the body of Jewish knowledge which we consider desirable for our children could easily be acquired in Sabbath schools. But there is too large an amount of subject matter to master. The vast majority of Israelites here are of German stock, and nearly every Israelite father wants and requires—rightly so—that children in school be taught not only English but also basic German and, secondarily, Hebrew. However, if the boys and girls are to be so advanced that at the close of their school years they have fully mastered two languages, English and German, and the third, Hebrew, understand well enough so that the Hebrew portions of our liturgy do not seem alien, and the easier books of the Bible are practically comprehensible in their original tongue, then we must establish for them such institutions in which this goal is attainable.

In a Sabbath school where the Jewish children assemble once weekly, this given goal cannot be reached, especially when, as is the case in the American cities on account of the Jews having settled en masse, these Sabbath schools are overcrowded and pedagogic personnel and facilities do not exist in adequate quantity. One must review daily the subject matter of Jewish education, if it is to be paralleled by deeper teaching. Sabbath schools are [only] a command of necessity. Yes, Jewish day schools! Or many more day schools, in which the pupils will have the opportunity to acquire for themselves the desirable Jewish learning.[106]

Felsenthal's plea, alongside Wise's pronouncement, adumbrated the public school versus day school debate of nearly a century later. Felsenthal, obviously devoted to intensive Jewish learning, recognized that, for most German Jewish parents, German ranked ahead of Hebrew as an educational priority. For Felsenthal, educational separation was by no means an ideal, but the educated Jew needed to know far more than could be learned in any setting but an all-day school. Notwithstanding Felsenthal's case for Jewish day schools, by the 1860s all New York Jewish day schools had closed, as had such schools in Cleveland, Detroit, Cincinnati, and Newark, New Jersey. Not long after 1871, a school opened by the Hebrew Education Society of Philadelphia in 1851 under Isaac Leeser's inspiration dropped general studies and confined itself to Jewish studies after public school attendance. Several Jewish day schools had functioned in Chicago, the last of which shut its doors in 1874.[107] None of the Jewish day schools established during the period under consideration survived through the 1870s.[108] Having embraced public education, Jewish leaders and the press kept close track of sectarianism in the schools to ensure that schools remained religiously neutral.[109]

By 1880, "Sabbath schools," meeting one or two days a week—Saturday afternoon and/or Sunday morning—and private lessons were the prevailing forms of Jewish education, although Talmud Torah schooling had made its appearance in America. Sabbath school was generally of three to five years' duration. The curriculum consisted of religious thought through catechism, Bible stories, and a few Hebrew verses for liturgical use. Synagogue-based, the Sabbath school aimed in part to prepare participants to share in the religious life of the congregation. The synagogue connection and attendant Hebrew curriculum distinguished such Sabbath schools from the earlier Philadelphia model. Rabbis typically served as superintendents, and volunteers—who often lacked substantial Jewish knowledge themselves—taught the classes at these very part-time schools. In 1874, Dr. Max Lilienthal initiated publication of *The Hebrew Sabbath School Visitor,* the first Jewish children's magazine in America, as an instructional aid for students in Sabbath school.[110] Notwithstanding its avowed inclination to traditionalism, Philadelphia's Sunday school used Lilienthal's magazine, the only available product of its kind.[111]

In a paper titled "Pedagogics in the Sabbath-School," presented in 1880, HUC professor Moses Mielziner reported that of 118 congregations affiliated with the Union of American Hebrew Congregations, only twelve did not operate a Sabbath school.[112] Mielziner observed that "it is the aim and object of our Sabbath-schools to impart to our children the necessary knowledge of the doctrines, the history and institutions of Judaism, to make them firm in adherence to our religious community, susceptible of religious devotion, strong for life's struggles and temptations, and conscious of their duties as men, citizens and Israelites."[113] Accordingly, a Sabbath school student between nine and fourteen years of age should become grounded in and knowledgeable of "the religious and moral doctrines of Judaism, biblical and postbiblical history, Hebrew reading and translation . . . and [a curricular enhancement urged by Mielziner] religious song."[114] A tall order for perhaps 800 hours of elementary school education! In the sphere of Hebrew language education, an area of learning in which Mielziner, a European-educated Talmud scholar, was a master, even the optimistic Mielziner could propose nothing beyond the rudimentary skills of mechanical Hebrew reading and translation.

Isaac Mayer Wise contemplated five years of religious school instruction, with the Bible as the school's principal textbook. Affirming that Hebrew is essential to the preservation of Judaism and to a correct understanding of the Bible, Wise averred that "the Hebrew language must be the principal study in Hebrew religious schools, to occupy two-thirds of the time; and the balance to be equally divided between Catechism and History."[115] Having initially supported the creation of day schools before embracing the model of public schools for general education, with part-time religious instruction in Jewish schools, Wise remained committed to a very substantial, though perhaps unrealistic—given a reduced instructional framework—course of study.[116]

Wise captured the prevailing sensibilities of American Jewry in the 1870s in declaring: "Judaism, in its doctrines and duties, is eminently humane, universal, liberal and progressive; in perfect harmony with modern science, criticism, and philosophy, and in full sympathy with universal liberty, equality, justice and charity."[117] This "at oneness" with America left open a compelling answer to the question of Jewish distinctiveness. Indeed, Wise's optimism must have been somewhat tempered by two symbolically significant events of 1876–78. First, Felix Adler, son of the rabbi of Temple Emanu-El of New York, renounced Judaism—after having studied for the rabbinate in Germany—in favor of "Ethical Culture," an ethics-based universalistic faith that he promoted. Second, Isaac Mayer Wise's daughter, Helen, eloped with a Presbyterian; the couple was married by a Unitarian minister. If Judaism was so much in harmony with universal principles, what—in the progressive, Western world—was its abiding uniqueness?

One hundred years after the founding of the American nation, the country's 250,000 Jews, primarily immigrants or descendants of immigrants from German-speaking lands, had a keen sense of belonging, abetted by the conviction that Judaism and Americanism were eminently compatible. Indeed, Jewish education was not merely Jewish; it was an expression of American ideals. Concomitantly, public education was the very symbol of America's great promise of inclusion. While the Catholic Church set up a system of parochial schools, Jews became champions of universalist, public education.

By 1880, Jewish education was increasingly accessed by enrolling one's child in a part-time religious school—most typically, a synagogue-connected Sabbath school. The fact that most congregations sponsored some type of religious school represented movement toward the notion of a communal stake in the Jewish education of successive generations. Public schools were seen as the appropriate setting for children's general education, though they needed to be vigilantly monitored for religious teaching. The home and synagogue or church, argued Jewish leaders, were the proper venues for Bible study.

There was not a professional cadre of Jewish educators. Sunday school teachers were chiefly volunteers, with limited knowledge of Jewish sources; hence, for example, the title of Wise's manual *The Essence of Judaism for Teachers and Pupils, and for Self-Instruction*. As for the rabbinic superintendents, no rabbi had yet been trained and ordained in America. Leeser, the traditionalist, and Felsenthal, the religious reformer, represented the minority view that the basic texts of Judaism required time on task that extended significantly beyond the bounds of possible attainment in a part-time religious school.

Frameworks of Jewish educational activity had expanded to include literary associations and then YMHAs. A stream of Eastern European immigrants had initiated Talmud Torah schools not attached to a particular congregation. A rabbinical seminary had been established and taken root.

In a letter presented to George Washington at the time of the Constitutional Convention, Jonas Phillips, a leading member of Shearith Israel of New York, had asked that there be no religious discrimination under the federal constitution that was being drafted. He added: "I solicit this favor for myself, my children and posterity, and for the benefit of all the Israelites through the thirteen United States of America."[118] One century later, Jews in America were flourishing economically and were more at home in America. If, however, Judaism and Americanism were so much at one, what was to make Judaism distinctive and compelling? What was, and who would teach, the essence of Judaism? Could or should Hebrew language be taught or emphasized? These were among the issues being discussed and debated by those Jews awakened to concern for the future of Jews qua Jews in the United States, as a new wave of mass migration began—a tidal wave that would see American Jewry grow from 250,000 in 1880 to 1 million by 1900 and 4 million by 1925.

CHAPTER THREE
Educational Trends at a Time of Mass Migration, 1881–1910

Though Eastern European Jews had been among the new arrivals to the United States in earlier generations, a massive wave of such immigrants came to American shores beginning in 1881. The new immigration resulted not only from pogroms and political persecution but from lack of economic opportunity. Over the nineteenth century, despite emigration, there was a fivefold increase in Eastern European Jewish population, exacerbating the struggle to earn a livelihood. While Eastern Europe was the primary source of Jewish immigration, Jews came from a diversity of lands. In addition to Ashkenazic newcomers, 30,000 Jews came to America from the Balkans, Turkey, and Greece early in the twentieth century. By 1910, swelled by immigration, the population of Jews in the United States had grown to 2 million.

Many of the new arrivals sought to balance the often conflicting claims of religious tradition, economic aspirations, and utopian ideologies. They represented, in the main, folk religious adherence; they were not the religious elites of the communities they left. Concern for the religious education of the next generation, however, gave rise to a brisk business in *hadarim*—privately run, one-room "instructional centers"— and a proliferation of Talmud Torah communal supplementary schools. A number of day schools were initiated, but they were a very marginal phenomenon before World War II. A community crisis in New York— home to one-third of America's Jews in 1880 and 44 percent by 1927— was to precipitate a significant communal initiative to systematically organize Jewish education early in the twentieth century.

The immigrants' readiness to enroll their children in public schools expressed, in part, their interest in adjusting to American life. Moreover, the established Jewish population had no interest in sponsoring Jewish day schools, and the immigrants lacked the resources to consider such an option. By 1905, on the Lower East Side of New York, thirty-eight elementary schools, serving a total population of 65,000 students, included 60,000 Jews.[119] An article in the July 1898 *Atlantic Monthly* reported that at least 500 of 1,677 students then at City College, where tuition and books were free, were Russian Jewish immigrants.[120]

While Jewish population in the United States was increasing substantially through immigration, the marriage and childbearing patterns of the longer-established, more acculturated American Jews evidenced a prospective looming challenge. In 1907, anthropologist Maurice Fishman reported a lower birthrate, fewer and later marriages, and more mixed marriages among Americanized Jews. But for immigration, Fishman wrote, the number of Jews "would dwindle away at a rate appalling to those who have the interests of their faith at heart."[121]

Notwithstanding its own acculturating trends, the established Jewish community undertook to assist the newcomers both materially and through Americanization initiatives. Such efforts included the provision of special classes in English and civics, often accompanied by an attempt to wean the Eastern European immigrants from the use of Yiddish. In some of the Jewish settlement houses, the use of Yiddish was prohibited. One of the largest of the newly established such organizations was the Educational Alliance, created by prominent New York Jews in 1893 as a vehicle of Americanization and social welfare.

For the acculturated descendants of German Jews, particularly women, benevolence was a primary focus of Jewish religious expression. Congregational sisterhoods, established late in the nineteenth century, actively participated in settlement activity. For such volunteers, settlement work was a Jewish religious experience. As one Denver woman wrote in 1906: "While we bring to them Americanism, we may at the same time be inspired with some of the spiritual passion which glows in the breasts of these ardent Jews, who are after all the rock which is the foundation of the House of Israel."[122]

A Jewish Awakening

Concomitant with the onset of mass migration was an awakening in Jewish life among young American-born Jews who, by the late 1870s, had lost confidence in the liberal, universalist visions of the era. Initiatives for the revitalization of Jewish education represented an expression of this awakening.[123] One such initiative, launched in 1893, was the Jewish Chautauqua Society, founded by Henry Berkowitz, one of four men in the first graduating class of HUC. Berkowitz, who participated in the creation of the Hebrew Sunday School Union in 1886, had also served as an editor of the weekly *Sabbath Visitor* and had helped compile *Bible Ethics* and the *Union Hebrew Reader* for use in Sunday schools.[124]

The Chautauqua Society, with a summer assembly at Lake Chautauqua, New York, had been created by Bishop John H. Vincent of the Methodist Episcopal Church in 1874. Initially developed as an intensive training program for Sunday school teachers, the society established adult correspondence courses and local reading circles. By the 1880s, it had become a forum for the discussion of literature, economics, science, politics, and religion. Dozens of local Chautauqua assemblies were formed; thus, Rabbi Berkowitz's initiative in creating the Jewish Chautauqua Society in Philadelphia—where he occupied the pulpit at Rodeph Shalom—was also part of a national phenomenon.[125]

Unlike other Chautauqua groups, the Jewish Chautauqua Society began with a Young Folks Reading Union for post-confirmation students. Jewish teens were offered four rationales for joining the group: "That they may become Jews by conviction, and not by inheritance. That they may see the history of the Jews in its relation to the development of civilization. That they may answer intelligently questions put to them by classmates, or others, about their faith and its history. That they make the history of today purer and nobler, with their own lives, through a study of the devotion and heroism of the Jewish fathers."[126] Berkowitz aimed to foster Jewish pride and, in the face of rising social anti-Semitism, to share the wisdom of the Jewish heritage.

The Jewish Chautauqua Society held its first summer assembly in 1894; by 1908, it had 125 circles, with 2,500 members. Beginning in 1909, it sent instructors to universities to teach summer courses on Jewish topics; this function was, by the 1930s, to become the society's central activity.[127] In 1915, the Jewish Chautauqua Society started a correspondence school as a means of strengthening Jewish education.

As reflected in the Chautauqua Society's Young Folks Reading Union, the Jewish education of children was a significant concern of the Jewish awakening. Indeed, the first publication of the newly established Jewish Publication Society, in 1890, was a revised edition of a book initially published in England by British children's author Lady Katie Magnus, titled *Outlines of Jewish History*. The JPS edition, which was available for use by Sabbath school instructors, among others, sold tens of thousands of copies and went through numerous printings.[128]

Jonathan Krasner observes that this work's negative images of Christianity and historical portrayal of Christians as fanatics may have resonated particularly with Reform Jewish leaders of the period. Jewish continuity seemed threatened by Unitarians, the Society of Ethical Culture, and liberal Protestant groups. Earlier generations' emphasis on Bible stories and on God's lovingkindness had, it seemed, been insufficient to make the case for Jewish uniqueness. Negative characterization of the "other" through history was one means of affirming and validating Jewish distinctiveness.[129]

Transplanted and Transformed

Eastern European Models of Jewish Education

Though immigrant Eastern European Jews did not attend German Jewish Sabbath schools, for many immigrant families Jewish education of the young was not entirely neglected. *Hadarim* (singular, *heder*; literally, "room")—a private, part-time Jewish educational enterprise—existed by the hundreds. The curriculum consisted, in the main, of rudimentary Hebrew reading, some *Humash* (Pentateuch), and synagogue skills. These *hadarim,* which were operated as businesses, often by persons of modest qualifications, achieved limited results. In the Old Country, there had been some communal control over Jewish education, but the absence of Jewish communal oversight, combined with the fact that parents had to focus on earning a living, left *heder* operators on their own.

The Talmud Torah, also a transplant from Eastern Europe—where it had served as a school for the children of the poor—was a parallel educational alternative. These communal schools, funded by very modest tuition and private contributions, were typically established in densely settled working- and lower-middle-class Jewish neighborhoods in urban areas. The course of study at most Talmud Torah schools approximated that of the Eastern European elementary *heder*: Hebrew reading—with particular attention to mechanical reading of the prayer book; translation into Yiddish, word by word, of the *Humash*; and the commentary of the medieval exegete Rashi on the *Humash*.[130]

In Eastern Europe, the elementary *heder*—which, unlike most American Talmud Torah schools, was restricted to boys—was designed to enable all males to meet the religious obligations associated with reciting prayers and reading Torah. Such *hadarim* typically had communal supervision. The American Talmud Torah schools were, in many cases, poorly organized and—though offering instruction most days of the week—did not always seat the same students. Rabbi Shemaryahu Leib Hurwich of the Salanter Talmud Torah stated that "our Talmud Torahs are like streetcars, always full but never with the same people."[131]

Since the American Talmud Torah was not exclusively a program for children of the poor, it attracted the close attention of those most interested in intensive Jewish education for children; some Talmud Torah schools provided a systematic program of study. During the years before and immediately after World War I, Talmud Torahs were established in Baltimore, Boston, Buffalo, Chicago, Cincinnati, Cleveland, Detroit, Indianapolis, Minneapolis, and Philadelphia, as well as in New York.[132] Among the teachers in the emergent Talmud Torahs were nationalistic Jews influenced by the Russian Haskalah (enlightenment) and Hibbat Zion (Love of Zion) movements.

Rabbi Moses Weinberger, who had but recently arrived in the United States from his native Hungary, described the state of Jewish education in New York City:

> There is nothing in the way of schooling here for the young men of Israel. Our faithful Orthodox brethren, who pride themselves on not seeking reforms, and revel in their own piety and righteousness, unhesitatingly allow their sons to grow up without Torah or faith. . . . And during the time when the Hungarian or Polish Jewish youngster was brought to a level where he could understand the Prophets, and listen to rigorous biblical and legal studies, the American youngster is merely brought to the magnificent level of being able to stammer a few words of English-style Hebrew to pronounce the blessing over the Torah, and to chant half the *maftir* [the weekly prophetic portion] from a text with vowels and notes on the day he turns thirteen—a day that is celebrated here as the greatest of holidays among our Jewish brethren.[133]

The bar mitzvah–focused Jewish education, evident in the days of Gershom Seixas, and later in the mid-nineteenth-century world of Isaac Leeser, was carried forward by Eastern European arrivals. In the face of this bleak picture, Weinberg was encouraged by the news of the opening of a yeshiva, Etz Chaim, for the study of Mishnah and Talmud.

Indeed, 1886 marked the organization of Yeshivat Etz Chaim, an all-day Jewish school for elementary school boys in New York. Launched by a group of supporters organized as Hebra Machzikei Yeshivat Etz Chaim (Association of the Supporters of Yeshivat Etz Chaim), the new day school rejected the prevailing trend of relegating Jewish study to "after school" hours. Even the most effective Talmud Torah program—and those who initiated Yeshivat Etz Chaim seem to have been supporters of the well-established Machzikei Talmud Torah—could not provide advanced Talmud instruction. Moreover, any form of supplementary Jewish schooling positioned the Americanizing public school as a central influence in children's education and socialization.[134] The school's constitution proclaimed: "The purpose of this Academy shall be to give free instruction to poor Hebrew children in the Hebrew language and the Jewish religion—Talmud, Bible, and *Shulhan Arukh*— during the whole day from nine in the morning until four in the afternoon. Also from four in the afternoon, two hours shall be devoted to teach the native language, English, and one hour to teach Hebrew— *loshon hakodesh*—and jargon [Yiddish] to read and write. The Academy shall be guided according to the strict Orthodox and Talmudic law and the custom of Poland and Russia."[135] The general studies program also included reading, spelling, grammar, and arithmetic. Among the school's students in the early 1890s was Mordecai Kaplan, who was to play an important role in Jewish educational developments in the decades ahead.[136] Though called a yeshiva, this elementary school, like others later to be established, differed significantly from its European predecessors, both because of the young age of its students and the inclusion of general education in its curriculum.

In the decades ahead, additional yeshiva schools, including the Rabbi Jacob Joseph Yeshiva (1900), the Yeshiva Rabbi Chaim Berlin (1906), and the Talmudical Institute of Harlem (1908) were established.[137] These day schools, however, remained a marginal phenomenon on the landscape of American Jewish education. To serve the continuing Jewish educational needs of Etz Chaim graduates and of more recent arrivals at advanced levels of Talmudic study, the Rabbi Isaac Elchanan Theological Seminary (RIETS) was founded by a group of Eastern European immigrants in 1897. Named for the recently deceased head of a famous yeshiva in Kovno, Rabbi Isaac Elchanan Spektor—who had ordained one of the RIETS founders, Rabbi Moses

Mayer Matlin—the new institution's aims were "to promote the study of Talmud and to assist in educating and preparing students of the Hebrew Faith for the Hebrew Orthodox Ministry."[138] A newspaper announced: "A daily *shiur* will be taught by a Rosh Yeshiva and a teacher will give instructions in the language of the land."[139] In its initial years, most RIETS students were Eastern European immigrants, aged eighteen to thirty.[140] RIETS combined with Yeshivat Etz Chaim in 1915; Etz Chaim was to become a high school, with RIETS devoted to more mature students pursuing ordination.

Founding of the Jewish Theological Seminary

On a parallel, though quite independent, track, established "Americanized" traditionalists banded together to create a more traditional seminary than HUC, in response to the perceived radical reform bent of the Hebrew Union College and its supporters. HUC had celebrated the school's first rabbinical students' graduation with a banquet featuring nonkosher food, and two years later a reform rabbinical gathering chaired by HUC president Isaac Mayer Wise issued the Pittsburgh Platform of 1885, a statement of guiding principles. Concomitantly, those who founded the new rabbinical school may have been reacting to the efforts of immigrant Eastern European Orthodox Jews to establish new mechanisms of rabbinical authority in America.[141] The effort to create what came to be called the Jewish Theological Seminary was spearheaded by Sabato Morais (1823–97), who had succeeded Isaac Leeser as hazzan of Mikveh Israel in Philadelphia. A native of Leghorn, Italy, Morais had served as school principal at the Bevis Marks congregation in London before being invited to Mikveh Israel.

The Pittsburgh Platform proclaimed, inter alia: "Today we accept as binding only the moral laws, and maintain only such ceremonies as elevate and sanctify our lives, but reject all such as are not adapted to the views and habits of modern civilization. . . . We consider ourselves no longer a nation, but a religious community. . . . We recognize in Judaism a progressive religion, ever striving to be in accord with the postulates of reason."[142] In contrast, the Jewish Theological Seminary, which opened in 1887, aimed at "the preservation in America of the knowledge and practice of historical Judaism." Its founders, in addition to Morais, included American-born, European-ordained rabbis Henry Schneeberger and Bernard Drachman, recently arrived Hungarian-born rabbi Alexander Kohut, and the British-born hazzan of New York's Shearith Israel, Henry Pereira Mendes.[143] In 1888, Morais reported to the Seminary board: "What the (modern rabbinical) seminaries at Breslau and Berlin, in Germany, at Budapest, in Hungary, at Rome, in Italy, are to Europe, this Jewish Theological Seminary should be to America."[144] While models of modern European Jewish seminaries informed those who founded JTS as well as those who had launched HUC, the men who created the Jewish Theological Seminary were traditional in their observance and united in their opposition to Reform. Seminary leadership included some who were Orthodox in outlook and practice; and some of a historical outlook who were more open to change in practice grounded in the evolving nature of halakhah (Jewish law).

Ambiguity as to the "practice of historical Judaism" was to be part of the ongoing debate among Seminary elites. It was several decades before it became clear that JTS represented something other than an Americanized Orthodoxy. Rabbi Joseph Hertz, the Seminary's first graduate, was to become the (Orthodox) chief rabbi of British Jewry. Rabbi Bernard Drachman, one of the founders of JTS and a member of its faculty for over twenty years, eventually joined the faculty of the (Orthodox) RIETS and Yeshiva College.

In the early years of the twentieth century, the Seminary received substantial funding from such well-established Reform Jews as Jacob Schiff, David Guggenheim, Louis Marshall, and Felix M. Warburg, who hoped that JTS would attract Russian Jewish students and prepare them to be leaders in the Americanization of immigrants.[145] Solomon Schechter, reader in rabbinics at Cambridge University, assumed the presidency of the fledgling Seminary in 1902. Under his leadership, JTS became both a center of Jewish scholarship and a core institution in the developing Conservative stream of Judaism.

Prior to Schechter's arrival, most of the Seminary's students were adolescents; Schechter created a junior division for those students who did not yet hold college degrees and a senior division for those who had earned a degree. By 1906, there were twenty-one students in the senior division.[146] The traditionalist Eastern European rabbis and students associated with RIETS were well aware of the growth and development of "Schechter's Seminary." In the winter of 1906, students at RIETS went on strike over the issue of secular education. They proclaimed: "We want to know Talmud and Codes better than the students of Schechter's Seminary. We want to know all the material that the rabbis of Russia do. But we want to have as much secular education as the students of Schechter's Seminary. We cannot be satisfied with the bit of English that the Administration permits us to study."[147] Bridging the divide between Eastern European Orthodoxy and the aspirations of Americanized, yet Orthodox, youth of Eastern European origin, was to become the task of Bernard Revel—future president of RIETS—described by Rabbi Moses S. Margolies, president of the Orthodox Agudat ha-Rabbanim, as "one of the Torah giants of our generation and perhaps the only one in general knowledge and science."[148] In 1909, Solomon Schechter opened the Teachers Institute (T.I.) of JTS, appointing Mordecai Kaplan, a Seminary rabbinical graduate, dean of the new department. In its first year, the Teachers Institute enrolled twenty-two women and twelve men.[149] The T.I. reflected the trends of professionalization and feminization well under way in public education at that time.

The Seminary's Teachers Institute was the second Jewish institution for the preparation of teachers in the United States. The first, Gratz College, had been launched in Philadelphia in 1893, through a bequest of Philadelphia merchant and philanthropist Hyman Gratz, brother of Rebecca Gratz. Both these teachers' colleges, like others that were subsequently established, were open to and attracted a significant number of women. This access to advanced Jewish study provided women with skills that enabled them to participate on an equal footing in Jewish life. Indeed, Jonathan Sarna suggests that "more than generally recognized, these teachers' colleges were the crucible of the Jewish feminist movement."[150]

Jewish Communal Responsibility for the Provision of Jewish Education

An organic process of Jewish educational development was under way, but it was an external event that served as the catalyst for a pivotal, communal educational initiative in New York City. In the September 1908 issue of *North American Review,* New York police commissioner Theodore A. Bingham wrote:

It is not astonishing that with a million Hebrews, mostly Russian, in the city (one quarter of the population) perhaps half of the criminals should be of that race when we consider that ignorance of the language, more particularly among men not physi-

cally fit for hard labor, is conducive to crime. . . . They are bur-
glars, firebugs, pickpockets and highway robbers—when they
have the courage; but though all crime is their province, pocket-
picking is the one to which they take most naturally. . . . Among
the most expert of all the street thieves are Hebrew boys who
are brought up to lives of crime. . . . The juvenile Hebrew emu-
lates the adult in the matter of crime percentage.[151]

This accusation galvanized hundreds of New York Jewish organizations—synagogues, federations, fraternal lodges, and professional societies—into collective action, resulting in the establishment of the New
York Kehillah in 1909.

The Kehillah was headed by Oakland-born, HUC-ordained Judah
Magnes, then rabbi at New York's Temple Emanu-El. Magnes was the
brother-in-law of the prominent Louis Marshall and was close to the
premier German Jewish banking families who were the leaders of
Emanu-El. He was attracted to the Yiddish intellectual milieu of the
Lower East Side Russian immigrants, and he enjoyed a broad-based following among the newcomers to America.

One response to the police commissioner's charge was the creation
by the Kehillah of the Committee on Jewish Education, charged with
surveying the state of Jewish education and developing appropriate responses to such needs as would be identified. The survey was undertaken by Professor Mordecai Kaplan of the Jewish Theological
Seminary and Dr. Bernard Cronson, a public school principal. The report identified six basic frameworks within which Jewish education was
being conducted: Talmud Torah schools, institutional schools, congregational schools, Sunday schools, *hadarim,* and private tutors.

The Talmud Torah schools, the researchers opined, "instill more
Jewishness into the lives of the children" than any of the other educational settings, despite the fact that "homework is never allotted; the
discipline is poor; the attendance is very irregular and seldom kept up
for any length of time."[152] The institutional schools, typically sponsored
by orphan asylums and social work agencies—often supported by German Jewish charitable groups—had the benefit of good pedagogy and
materials but lacked the confidence of the population they aimed to
serve, because the intended beneficiaries "do not regard it as Jewish
enough insofar as it makes Hebrew only secondary."[153] Congregational
schools, holding sessions three or more times a week, were generally
connected to a Conservative or an Orthodox synagogue. Here, "the

work covered is not very extensive, and is usually confined to the reading and translation of the prayers, and of a few passages in the Bible,
with a smattering of a few rules of grammar."[154] Sunday schools, reported the survey, engaged a cadre of public school teachers, mostly
women, many of whom volunteered their services. However, these
teachers lacked "the knowledge necessary for a Jewish school" and carried out "a vague kind of curriculum."[155] As to the *heder*, the researchers were unsparingly critical:

> A *heder* is a school conducted by one, two or three men, for the
> sole purpose of eking out some kind of livelihood which they
> failed to obtain by any other means. It generally meets in a
> room or two, in the basement or upper floor of some old dilapi-
> dated building where the rent is at a minimum. . . . The instruc-
> tion, which seldom goes beyond the reading of the prayer book,
> and the teaching of a few blessings by rote, is carried on only in
> Yiddish. The method of instruction is quite unique. It consists
> of about fifteen minutes of individual instruction, with seldom
> or never any class work. Each pupil, not knowing when he is
> needed, straggles in at random, and waits for his turn to come,
> in the meantime entertaining himself with all sorts of mischief.
> When his turn comes and the teacher has given him the fifteen
> minutes, he runs off. There is hardly an ideal aim in the mind of
> the teacher, except in some cases it is the training for the Bar
> Mitzvah feat of reading the Haftorah.[156]

With regard to private tutors, gauging their number is "not amenable to
investigation," reported the survey.[157] The data showed total enrollment
of 41,000 students in the Talmud Torahs; the institutional, congregational, and Sunday schools; and the various *hadarim*. The number of
Jewish children of school age receiving any form of Jewish education in
all the frameworks identified was estimated at 21–24 percent. This
snapshot of Jewish education in New York City reflected, albeit on a
grander scale, the profile of Jewish educational opportunities in other
locales.[158]

Ready to initiate communal action to address these challenges, the
New York Kehillah developed a strategic approach that was to be replicated in the decades ahead in dozens of American Jewish communities. It
established the Bureau of Jewish Education. The BJE, launched through
a $50,000 contribution from Jacob Schiff and $25,000 from the New

York Foundation (a fund administered by the banking firm of Kuhn, Loeb and Company), was initially to perform the following functions:

1. To study sympathetically and at close range all the Jewish educational forces in New York City, including alike those that restrict themselves to religious instruction and those that look primarily to the Americanization of our youth, with a view to cooperation and the elimination of waste and overlapping.
2. To become intimately acquainted with the best teachers and workers who are the mainstay of these institutions, and organize them for both their material and their spiritual advancement.
3. To make propaganda through the Jewish press and otherwise, in order to acquaint parents with the problem before them and with the means for solving it.
4. To operate one or two model schools for elementary pupils, for the purpose of working out the various phases of primary education, these schools to act also as concrete examples and guides to now existing Hebrew schools, which will undoubtedly avail themselves of the textbooks, methods, appliances, etc. worked out in the model schools.[159]

Consistent with the prevailing spirit of progressivism, identifying the problem and creating systems and order were, presumably, the essential starting points for improvement.

Dr. Samson Benderly, consultant to the Kehillah on the Kaplan-Cronson survey and its analysis, was engaged by Magnes and the Kehillah board as director of the new bureau. Benderly's ideas, which were to shape the work of the New York bureau and influence scores of Jewish educators summoned to leadership in communities throughout the country, grew out of his experiences in Palestine and the United States and in the context of progressive education and Zionist thought. Born in Safed, Benderly traveled at age fifteen to Beirut to study at the American University. After completing a B.A., he began medical studies. In 1898, Dr. Aaron Friedenwald, professor of ophthalmology in Baltimore, visited Beirut, and in an encounter with Benderly, encouraged the aspiring medical student to come to the United States. By September 1898, Benderly had moved to Baltimore, where he completed his medical studies at the College of Physicians and Surgeons. Concurrently, he undertook to teach Hebrew and direct a Jewish school.[160] The time demands of medical residency eventually forced Benderly to choose between medicine and Jewish education; he chose the latter.

Benderly's program of Hebrew immersion included not only Hebrew language but also Bible, holidays, history, and activities designed to nurture strong connection to the Land of Israel. In 1905, he initiated a youth group called "Herzl's Children." He used visual aids and used music, dance, and drama as instructional tools. Benderly was certain that Jewish education was essential to the survival of the Jewish people in the United States and that, to be successful with the Americanized children of immigrants, it needed to take on new forms. One enthusiastic observer wrote: "The educational program of Dr. Benderly . . . is the only answer to Jewish education in America. Benderly has integrated Jewish education into the needs and requirements of the American environment. He has shown his pedagogic genius."[161]

After starting his Baltimore career at a synagogue school, Benderly took a position as head of the Hebrew Free School for Poor and Orphaned Children. Early in his Baltimore stay, Benderly served as Hebrew tutor to his patron Dr. Friedenwald's son, Harry, then in his thirties. The younger Friedenwald was to become president of the Federation of American Zionists, later known as the Zionist Organization of America. At the same time, Benderly tutored Henrietta Szold, then in her forties, who was soon to found Hadassah.[162] Benderly's educational approach, centering on children and the development of a school-based society, was anchored in the progressive education ideals of John Dewey.

Benderly's Zionist-nationalist orientation, emphasizing Hebrew and a connection to Palestine, was well known to the Kehillah committee that enlisted him, and most of those responsible for overseeing the bureau identified with this direction. The executive committee to which Benderly reported in New York consisted of five individuals, four of whom were Zionists: Israel Friedlaender, Judah Magnes, Mordecai Kaplan, and Henrietta Szold. The fifth, Louis Marshall, was close to Jacob Schiff and was likely keeping a watchful eye on the project for Schiff.

Modern Zionism had, by 1910, expressed itself in two *aliyot*—waves of emigration—to Palestine, several Zionist Congresses, and a wide range of Zionist ideologies. For Benderly and his committee, it was the cultural Zionism of Ahad Ha'am (the pen name of Asher Zvi Ginsberg) together with a commitment to Americanism that shaped an approach to Jewish education. As Judah Magnes, borrowing from Ahad Ha'am, phrased it: "If in the lands of oppression, the Jews be held in bodily bondage, in the lands of freedom all too many are spiritual slaves." Zionism's task was "to make Jews free in body and spirit."[163]

In the modern era, the Zionist center in Palestine would, it was imagined, serve as a hub of renewed Jewish cultural creativity, sustaining
Jewish life in the diaspora.

Just as Western European emancipation provided the context for
the reform of Judaism, the apparent failure of integration into Western
host countries or of security within culturally diverse Eastern European
nations fueled a quest for normalizing Jewish existence in the modern
era by a renewal of vibrant Jewish life in the Land of Israel. From the
outset, the Zionist movement was composed of multiple strands. Political Zionism, labor Zionism, socialist Zionism, and religious Zionism
were among the ideologies represented in the thinking and practical activities of the developing movement, before and after the First Zionist
Congress convened by Herzl in 1897.

Ahad Ha'am, who participated in the First Zionist Congress,
doubted whether Zionism could solve the social, economic, or political
challenges of the Jews. He believed, however, that love of Zion represented an answer to the problem of Judaism. Throughout the lands of
their dispersion, Jews were assimilating. In the modern era, religion was,
for growing numbers of Jews, no longer a sustaining force. Ahad Ha'am
was convinced that a Jewish community in the Land of Israel, grounded
in Jewish national consciousness and a renewal of Hebrew creativity,
could serve as a spiritual center, connecting and nurturing diaspora communities. As Ahad Ha'am saw it, culture in the modern world expresses
itself through the national spirit. As Jews left the ghetto, they could not
maintain Jewish culture; rather, they became absorbed into the dominant
environment. Thus, Judaism was in a quandary; "its life is in danger."
The need of the age was, for Ahad Ha'am,

> the creation in its native land of conditions favorable to its de-
> velopment: a good-sized settlement of Jews working without
> hindrance in every branch of civilization; from agriculture and
> handicrafts to science and literature. This Jewish settlement,
> which will be a gradual growth, will become in course of time
> the center of the nation, wherein its spirit will find pure expres-
> sion and develop in all its aspects to the highest degree of per-
> fection of which it is capable. Then, from this center, the spirit
> of Judaism will radiate to the great circumference, to all the
> communities of the Diaspora, to inspire them with new life and
> to preserve the over-all unity of our people.[164]

Those primarily responsible for the BJE embraced this ideology. They saw the challenge of the new, communal Jewish educational mechanism—whose curriculum would be closely connected to the cultural awakening in Palestine—as a sustaining support lever for Jewish life in America. Benderly was convinced that American Jews needed to find a way to integrate into their environment while maintaining Jewish distinctiveness. In an era in which cultural pluralism was—at least among intellectual elites—identified as a strength of the American republic, educating American Jews to strong identification with national Hebrew culture was seen as complementary to—and indeed, an expression of—Americanism. As Louis Brandeis, later to be appointed to the United States Supreme Court, said of American Zionism in 1915: "Indeed, loyalty to America demands rather [than otherwise] that each American Jew become a Zionist. For only through the ennobling effect of its strivings can we develop the best that is in us and give to this country the full benefit of our inheritance."[165] Though confident that the Zionist revival in the Land of Israel would become a vital source of spiritual energy, Benderly realistically noted that the combination of cultural Zionism and state-of-the-art instructional techniques could not guarantee universal Jewish continuity in the dispersion.[166]

The American milieu, Benderly affirmed, called for a particular educational framework—"the double school system. We must have a system of Hebrew schools which our children can attend after their daily attendance in the public schools."[167] Such a system would nurture "the growth and development of a normal Jewish life in harmony with modern civilization."[168] Inspired by Ahad Ha'am and by John Dewey's vision of the school as a social center, Benderly saw part-time communal Jewish schools, rather than synagogues, as spiritual centers for American Jewish life. Benderly's Hebraist-Zionist approach implicitly rejected the educational emphases of Orthodoxy and Reform.

Close collaboration ensued between Benderly and Mordecai Kaplan. Benderly sought trained personnel, and Kaplan's T.I. aimed to provide educational training. Benderly encouraged a group of young men to pursue doctorates at Columbia University's Teachers College, while studying Judaica and pedagogy at the T.I. He was convinced that the development of a professional educator corps would be better advanced by pedagogical training than by rabbinic study. The T.I. program, which served as a model for Hebrew teachers' colleges across the country, rested on four foundations:

1. Jewish language—Hebrew and its modern literature
2. Jewish religion—as defined by the Bible and its interpretation
3. Jewish history—postbiblical and contemporary
4. Jewish education—the art and science of teaching.[169]

Yet, even as Kaplan cooperated with Benderly, he was uneasy with the latter's exclusive emphasis on the national aspect of Jewish culture, noting in his journal that "only by giving Jewish culture a distinctively religious significance in the true modern sense of the term is there any hope of Jewish education being built up in this country."[170]

By the close of the generation of 1881–1910, three major rabbinical training institutions had taken root in American soil. An awakening of Jewish interest was manifest among elements of the more established adult Jewish population, expressed, inter alia, in the establishment and resonance of the Jewish Chautauqua Society and the Jewish Publication Society. Though they were by no means of broad appeal, several yeshiva day schools were created by Eastern European immigrants. Each of these day schools included general education as an integral part of the curriculum. For the most part, until 1910, Jewish education was left by the new immigrants to private arrangements—with *hadarim* the prevalent, though not exclusive, framework for the education of children. The New York Kehillah, a voluntary umbrella association of Jewish organizations, undertook an initiative of tectonic significance by establishing the Bureau of Jewish Education, expressing thereby a Jewish communal responsibility for Jewish education. The vehicle that BJE director Samson Benderly and his supporters saw as best suited to furthering Jewish consciousness, learning, and commitment to Jewish ideals was the Talmud Torah afternoon school, and it was to creating and strengthening a communal Talmud Torah system that the new bureau promptly turned its attention.

CHAPTER FOUR

Institutional Development, 1910–45

The period 1910–45 saw the growth and development of many of the Jewish educational frameworks that continue to serve Jews and nurture Jewish life in the twenty-first century. Not only Bureaus of Jewish Education but Jewish educational camps, youth groups, Hillel college campus organizations, Jewish community centers, and Jewish early childhood education centers made their appearance, and congregational afternoon schools as well as day schools were poised for major growth. The relocation to the United States of European Jewish refugees—200,000 during the period 1933–45—was to have significant impact in the years to follow.

The Talmud Torah Generation

The New York Bureau of Jewish Education, established as a vehicle for expanding and improving Jewish education in a growing community, initiated an aggressive program of federating and supporting Talmud Torah schools, providing in-service professional training to educators, writing modern textbooks, and recruiting pupils. Consistent with cultural Zionist ideals, the Talmud Torah curriculum promoted by the BJE was Hebrew-based. It included Hebrew language and literature, Bible, festivals, Palestine as the source of Jewish creativity, selections from rabbinic literature—primarily drawn from midrash and the Talmud—Jewish history, and a degree of synagogue ritual familiarity under the rubric "customs and ceremonies." The bureau encouraged the use of arts and crafts, music, and dramatics in the instructional program; each of these educational techniques represented an innovation at the time. The BJE also assembled graduates of the various Talmud Torahs and launched a Hebrew high school. The bureau established the Board of Teachers License and the Hebrew Principals Association. Recognizing the importance of "beyond the classroom" experiences, the BJE organized the League of Jewish Youth and opened a summer camp.

Consistent with educational progressivism, Samson Benderly advocated and imposed expert supervision in BJE-operated Talmud Torah schools. While his corps of close BJE associates were primarily male (known as "Benderly boys"), Benderly opened preparatory schools designed to train female students for such programs as that offered at the JTS Teachers Institute. The first three such schools were for girls only, and, by 1912, they collectively served more than 1,200 girls aged eleven to fifteen.[171] In fact, at least one of the early "Benderly boys" was female: Rebecca Aaronson. Aaronson, who studied at Columbia and at the Seminary's Teachers Institute, met "Benderly boy" Barnett Brickner—later to become a prominent Reform rabbi—in class, and they were married in 1919.[172] Throughout Rabbi Brickner's decades in the rabbinate, primarily in Cleveland, Rebecca Aaronson Brickner was to play a leading role as teacher, community organizer, lecturer, and *rebbetzin*.

An October 1914 journal entry by Mordecai Kaplan provides a glimpse at the close relationship between Benderly and his bureau and the Teachers Institute directed by Kaplan:

> Dr. B himself taught [a group of young men] Hebrew for two hours every morning during an entire summer. He had them read modern Hebrew literature and inculcated in them at the same time an enthusiasm for the general cause of Jewish education as he hoped to establish it. He also got a Dr. Shapiro to give them a more thorough grounding in grammar and composition. Later in the year about the middle of winter he asked me to give them some work and I took up with them the course in interpretation that I had been giving in the Institute to my regular classes. My work with that group did not constitute part of my duties at the Institute, but I carried it on for the Bureau. In June 1912 that group was turned over by the Bureau to the Teachers Institute. The work with them was then divided between Dr. Friedlaender and myself. He was to give them instruction in Bible and history and I was to give them the principles of Jewish education.[173]

Consistent with Benderly's *ivrit b'ivrit* (Hebrew in Hebrew) approach, the T.I. engaged a teaching faculty of Hebraists, and most course instruction was conducted in Hebrew. Starting in the 1920s, Kaplan—again, in keeping with and complementing the cultural emphasis of the Benderly program of Talmud Torah education—introduced arts to the Teachers Institute curriculum. Music and graphic arts faculty were part of the teaching corps, and performances of student dramatic productions were regularly held.[174]

The centrality of the Jewish educational agenda to the Kehillah that founded the bureau is reflected in the fact that, of the 1915 Kehillah budget of $108,493, the BJE received $68,064.[175] Notwithstanding this demonstration of its commitment to the work of the bureau as a communal priority, Benderly's creative zeal to do ever more programming sometimes led to charged encounters with the bureau's trustees. Zevi Scharfstein, who worked at the BJE for many years, reports that at a meeting at which several trustees were present, trustee Israel Friedlaender requested that Benderly balance income and expense. To this, Benderly replied: "You are one of the trustees of the bureau. Do you know what your job is? To listen to me. I am the master of the bureau."[176] Nonetheless, the accomplishments of the BJE were considerable, and the communal model initiated in New York was, in the three decades that followed, replicated in eighteen additional communities, coast to coast. Many of these central agencies were headed by "Benderly boys."[177]

One impediment to success in attracting a broad base of students to Talmud Torah schools was class consciousness. Upwardly mobile parents perceived the Talmud Torah as a philanthropic institution serving the poor, and, in fact, classes included scholarship recipients. As one board member observed: "Originally, when we started it was supposed to be a *balabotishe* [upscale] Hebrew school. It turned out that our *balabotim* [affluent members; literally, "house owners"] refused to send their children to this school."[178] As new Jewish neighborhoods were established in areas of second and third settlement, synagogues supplanted Talmud Torahs as school centers.

Although the New York Kehillah did not endure, the BJE that it had launched became affiliated with—and drew financial support from—New York's Federation for the Support of Jewish Philanthropic Societies in 1917. The New York Federation, like other emerging Jewish Federations across the country, accepted the communal investment in Jewish education without regard to the particular ideology articulated by the individual schools. The rationale for this approach was grounded, in part, on the pragmatic sense that providing such support would benefit the general campaign of the Jewish Federation:

> The application of religious schools for affiliation with Federation presents distinctly to Federation the problem of admitting societies carrying on religious education as distinguished from institutions engaged mainly in secular social work.
>
>   When the plan of Federation was adopted it was agreed to be unwise for the Federation to complicate its problems at the beginning by taking over the support of institutions engaged in philanthropic-religious activities. . . . In support of a modification of the Plan of Federation so as to embrace religious philanthropic endeavor, it is submitted by the School Committee that such a step will serve to unify the community and to win for Federation support for general charities from elements that have hitherto held aloof.[179]

The philanthropic aspect of the provision of religious education was emphasized: the committee was prepared to embrace support of the "religious instruction for those classes in the community unable to bear the expense."[180] Moreover, extending aid to Jewish education was undertaken with an eye to cultivating Federation financial support from Jews particularly dedicated to the cause of education. The Federation affiliated the BJE as well as some of the larger Talmud Torahs, enabling Benderly and the BJE to continue the array of initiatives.[181]

   Communal sponsorship and a Hebrew language emphasis—a cultural unifier—established the Talmud Torah as a community program. While not opposed to religious practice, the Hebrew language aims of the BJE Talmud Torah system were grounded in the cultural renewal envisioned by Ahad Ha'am, not in equipping students with synagogue skills. With few exceptions, Talmud Torah schools, like public schools and Sabbath schools, operated on a coeducational basis.[182] As in Sabbath schools and public schools, women were well represented in the teaching force. Benderly effectively encouraged scores of young American Jews—men and women—to study both education and Judaica, to prepare for careers as Jewish educators.

   Despite Benderly's affirmation of the desirability of the "double school system," there was, for many students, a fundamental disconnect between the two schools' curricula. Of his studies at the "Downtown Talmud Torah" on the Lower East Side from 1918 to 1924, Lewis Feuer wrote:

[A]t our Talmud Torah on Sunday mornings, we would sing songs from *The Jewish Songster*. . . . The Zionist songs, however, for most of us had a certain unreality as they all seemed to entail a return to Palestine, and we were all with rare exceptions, staunch American patriots.

When we reached the upper grades . . . we became aware that the militant prophets were always denouncing the Kings at Jerusalem, even King Solomon himself, for permitting the country people to make their sacrifices in their own local "high places" rather than making the journey to Jerusalem; they excoriated King Solomon for allowing foreign religions to establish their own places of worship in the great city. But we were learning at the same time in our public school that freedom of religious worship was the right of every American citizen.[183]

For Feuer, as for others like him, the Zionist-nationalist approach was not compelling and also not in keeping with American values. Trained pedagogues, a well-developed course of study, and use of the arts in Jewish education could not address the desire for Americanization or synthesize conflicting values.

Feuer's observations speak to the complexity and tension inherent in the challenge of adopting a vision for Jewish life in America and translating it into an effective educational program—a challenge for Benderly's generation as well as for those that have followed. Benderly was convinced that his vision and educational approach represented the formula for Jewish survival in America. While such needs as recruiting educators, addressing the relationship of Jews to one another and to society, and exploring innovative instructional strategies are ongoing, perhaps one lesson of the Benderly era is that no single vision or approach will meet the needs of diverse Jewish communities.

Schooling "On the Margins"

Secular Yiddish schools offered a significant alternative to Talmud Torah, *heder*, and Sunday schools. Starting in 1908, in Brownsville, New York—an area in Brooklyn with a large working-class population noted for socialist leanings—Yiddish schools of various kinds were established in every major center of Jewish population. Among the larger networks of Yiddish schools were those of the Arbeiter Ring (Work-men's Circle), grounded in secularism and radicalism. Their sponsors avowed that such schools were necessary because "in a capitalist society the public schools are controlled largely by capitalists, the enemies of the working class. . . . The teachers are forced to plant in the young innocent hearts reactionary chauvinism."[184] By 1922, there were forty-seven Workmen's Circle schools, the curricula of which included Jewish folk music, Yiddish literature, Jewish history, and history of the working class.[185] Similarly, Poale Zion, the American Labor Zionist movement, created a network of *folkshuln*—"schools for the people"—promoting Yiddish, as well as Hebrew, socialism, Jewish history, and those aspects of Judaism that lent themselves to translation into nationalist and socialist idioms. In addition to the ideological underpinnings of Yiddish schools, another rationale for such schools advanced by their advocates was that education in *Yiddishkeit,* the culture of the Eastern European immigrant parents, would bridge the divide between parents and their American-born children.[186] By the mid-1920s, the peak period of Yiddish secular education, 10,000 to 12,000 children attended *folkshuln,* which centered on the study of Yiddish.[187]

In 1917, the public schools of New York enrolled 277,000 Jewish students, while the city's Orthodox day schools enrolled one thousand.[188] Orthodox day schools continued to be established, albeit at a slow pace, in the second and third decades of the twentieth century. In 1928, 4,290 students were enrolled in seventeen such schools, considerably fewer than the number of students in secular Yiddish schools.[189] Between 1917 and 1939, four progressive Jewish day schools were established, among the twenty-three day schools launched in New York in those years.[190] The progressive institutions sought to synthesize progressive and Jewish education; limited time was devoted to Hebrew studies. Three of these schools closed their doors after brief periods of operation, for lack of pupils and financial support. The fourth of the progressive schools, Brandeis Bi-Cultural School, eventually affiliated with the Conservative movement.[191] Of the thirty day schools in the United States in 1939, twenty-seven were in New York, with the others in Baltimore; Dorchester, Massachusetts; and Union City, New Jersey.[192]

A noteworthy structural opportunity for part-time Jewish study presented itself, beginning in 1913, with the spread of the Gary Plan, initiated in Gary, Indiana. The Gary Plan, among other innovations, authorized off-campus release time during the school day for religious instruction. In New York, the plan was supported by the Reform movement and opposed by supporters of the Talmud Torah system. Reform educators were finding Sunday-only instruction insufficient to meet their Jewish educational goals; release time thus represented a potential slot for additional instructional time. The Gary Plan, on the other hand, lengthened the school day. Supporters of the five-day-a-week Talmud Torah—which drew children from multiple public schools—were concerned about the likely negative impact on scheduling and enrollment in the established, more intensive Jewish educational programs.[193]

Though the Gary Plan did not survive long, it elicited various pronouncements within the Jewish community on church-state considerations relating to education. For example, Isadore Montefiore Levy, a member of the New York City Board of Education, observed in 1915: "To revolutionize our system by the introduction of the religious feature would be to open the floodgate to a tide of possible bitterness and hatred. . . . [R]eligious denominations would sooner or later make our schools a battlefield upon which would be fought their ancient enmities."[194] Rabbi Samuel Schulman, a leading Reform rabbi and outspoken anti-Zionist in New York City, stated: "[O]ur purpose as Jews should be not merely the negative one of opposing the introduction of Bible reading in the public schools . . . but the . . . positive one of utilizing whatever methods are offered with which we can sympathize, which aim at improving the knowledge of the Bible and the general ethical and religious culture of the American nation."[195] Discussions of "strict separation" of church and state were to become a matter of considerable debate later in the twentieth century, regarding public funding in support of education in nonpublic schools—and early in the twenty-first century, as the first publicly funded charter school with a Hebrew emphasis opened in Florida. It was a debate with roots in the nineteenth century and, indeed, anchored in the inherent tension between the free exercise and establishment clauses of the First Amendment to the United States Constitution.

Nonformal Jewish Education

In 1913, many of the country's YMHAs and YWHAs—which had been established starting in 1888—organized to form the Council of Young Men's Hebrew and Kindred Associations. The Jewish Welfare Board (JWB), created in 1917 to provide Jewish chaplains and support services during World War I, helped meet the religious needs of Jews serving in the armed forces. The Ys cooperated with the JWB and, in 1921, the Council of Young Men's Hebrew and Kindred Associations merged with the JWB. Many mergers of YMHAs and YWHAs ensued, with most of the new institutions taking the name Jewish Community Center. In 1990, the national JWB itself was to be renamed the Jewish Community Centers Association of North America. The centers in the 1920s and 1930s inherited from the Ys a culture of Americanizing Russian Jewish newcomers.

The first Jewish residential camps date to the closing decade of the nineteenth century. A 1936 directory of Jewish camps sponsored by Jewish communal organizations listed eighty-eight such camps in the United States and Canada.[196] Fresh air camps, the earliest residential camps under Jewish sponsorship, emphasized Americanization and good health. Though serving Jewish constituents, they were inspired by the American camping ideals of the "back to nature" movement and of Progressivist thinking then in vogue and did not have a uniquely Jewish mission.

Jewish educational camping was launched in 1919, by Dr. Albert P. Schoolman. Schoolman, a disciple of Samson Benderly, founded Cejwin (Central Jewish Institute) camps, to use the summer months to strengthen the educational program of the Institute's Talmud Torah program. He was influenced by progressive educational thinking that recognized the possibilities for the individual and group development in camping. Though the boom period of Jewish educational camping was yet to come, Jewish camps of diverse ideologies, both communal and private, were operating in the 1920s and 1930s.[197] Among the educational camps of note were Camp Modin and Camp Achvah. Modin, modeled on Cejwin, was operated by three Benderly boys (Albert Schoolman, Isaac Berkson, and Alexander Dushkin) and their wives on a private basis and targeted wealthy clientele. Achvah was established by Samson Benderly as a Jewish educational leadership training camp.[198]

In the early years of Camp Achvah, started in 1927, Benderly recruited a group, Kvutzah, with the aim of developing career Jewish educators. Every aspect of camp life was carried on in Hebrew. As Kvutzah members recalled:

Everything was conducted in Hebrew—eating, studies, conversation, sports, dramatics, discussion. It was the first camp of its kind. The Habimah Theater made its appearance in America that year [1928], and with his usual zeal for ideas, Dr. Benderly immediately insisted that the mode of pronunciation be Sephardit. It was quite a hardship upon Dr. Benderly himself who spoke Sephardit with a strong Ashkenazic accent, but he persisted. The influence of Palestine was very strong, and it was constantly brought to the fore by Dr. Benderly.[199]

Aspects of Benderly's experiment—which suffered from the impact of the Depression—were to be further developed by others in the 1940s and 1950s. Cejwin, Modin, and Achvah—like Jewish educational camps later to be launched—had a profound impact on staff as well as on campers. Alumni of these camps were to be among the founders of a number of the post–World War II initiatives in Jewish educational camping.

In the early decades of the twentieth century, informal Jewish youth movements were formed, including such Zionist youth groups as Young Judaea (1909), Hashomer Hatza'ir (1923), AZA (1924), and Habonim Dror (1935).[200] The (Reform) North American Federation of Temple Youth (NFTY, 1939) and (Conservative) Leadership Training Fellowship (1945) followed suit. By 1940, there were thirty nationally organized American Jewish youth groups. Many served young people aged eighteen to twenty-five or thirty; only four—Young Israel, Agudat Israel Youth, Young Judaea, and Hashomer Hatza'ir—served children under twelve years of age.[201] Many Central and Eastern European Jews who came to the U.S. during the interwar period had been active in European Zionist youth movements, adding to the development of such groups in America.[202] Tabulation of membership in twenty-six of the thirty national Jewish youth organizations for 1939–40 showed 61,019 males and 99,262 females participating,[203] a ratio not unlike that at the close of the twentieth century in many of the nonformal Jewish programs serving Jewish teens and young adults.

As early as 1889, fifty of the 300 degree recipients at the tuition-free, all-female Hunter College were Jewish women.[204] As young immigrants and the children of immigrants began to attend college in greater numbers, Jewish campus organizations were founded. The Menorah movement began in 1906 with the establishment at Harvard University of the Harvard Menorah Society for the Study and Advancement of Jewish Ideals. Jewish student organizations were similarly launched at several other universities. In 1913, the Intercollegiate Menorah Association was organized at a convention held at the University of Chicago. The object of the IMA, as expressed in its constitution, was "the promotion in American colleges and universities of the study of Jewish his-

tory, culture, and problems, and the advancement of Jewish ideals."
Basic elements of any Menorah Society were lectures and study circles;
by 1917, there were more than sixty such societies.

Though constituting less than 4 percent of the U.S. population, Jews
accounted for 9 percent of college enrollment in the 1920s.[205] Jews on
campus—as elsewhere—often encountered social hostility and exclusion. On this backdrop, Hillel Centers, starting at the University of Illi-
nois in Champaign in 1923, were formed. Hillel, which encouraged
social and cultural as well as scholarly programs, was a setting that enabled students to comfortably interact with Jewish peers. Among the offerings that Hillel might provide would be a list of landlords who would
rent to Jewish students.[206] B'nai B'rith undertook sponsorship of Hillel
in 1925, and Hillel Centers were soon established at state universities in
Wisconsin, Ohio, West Virginia, California, and Texas, and at Cornell.
By the late 1920s, the Intercollegiate Menorah Association, which had
been characterized by a purely intellectual focus, ended, supplanted by
the more socially oriented Hillel Centers.

Teachers' Colleges and
National Educational Organizations

In addition to Gratz College and the Teachers Institute of JTS, institutions
for the education of Jewish teachers were established in New York, Baltimore, Boston, Pittsburgh, Cleveland, and Chicago between 1917 and
1929.[207] It was anticipated that the emerging communal Talmud Torah
system would require a full-time teaching corps; hence the need for Hebrew teachers' colleges. Moreover, these institutions were centers of
higher Jewish learning, and their instructors often saw their mission as ensuring the continuity of Jewish life in America. The founding of one such
Hebrew college offers a glimpse of prevailing realities and expectations.

In 1917, the twelve Hebrew schools of Boston joined together as the
Associated Boston Hebrew Schools. Within a year, the community's
Sunday schools united as the Bureau of Jewish Religious Schools. In
1920, the two associations merged as the Bureau of Jewish Education.
The superintendent of the BJE, Louis Hurwich, with the support of the
bureau board and of the Boston Federation of Jewish Charities, initiated
the establishment of the Hebrew Teachers College of Boston. In autumn
1921, the college opened with thirteen students, eight of whom had had

European *heder* education and five of whom were American-born graduates of Boston Hebrew schools. After a four-year course of study, twelve graduates received diplomas as teachers at the college's first commencement, in 1925; each graduate was immediately employed in the community's growing Hebrew school system.[208] The communal model of Talmud Torah education seemed headed for ascendancy in the American environment, and Hebrew teachers' colleges, it was anticipated, would train the necessary faculties for a growing educational system.

During the World War I era, Julius Greenstone, a professor at Gratz College, observed that two types of teachers were on the American Jewish educational scene: zealous American-educated teachers lacking in subject knowledge; and Jewishly knowledgeable teachers lacking sympathy with American conditions. While applauding the phenomenon of teachers' college graduates, Greenstone noted that "in order to make this new class of teachers extensive and permanent, it is essential that teaching in Jewish religious schools become an honorable profession, commanding the respect and appreciation of the community expressed in adequate remuneration."[209] Greenstone's plaint was to be echoed throughout the twentieth century and into the twenty-first.

As the teaching profession grew—in number of practitioners and level of training—several teachers' organizations were established, including the Hebrew Teachers Union.[210] To provide a forum for Jewish educational leaders and to bridge the efforts of communities across the country, the National Council for Jewish Education (NCJE) was established in 1926. This organization led to the creation in 1939 of the American Association for Jewish Education (AAJE) as a national service agency in Jewish education.[211] The AAJE linked Bureaus of Jewish Education that were, by that time, becoming educational service providers to synagogue schools, rather than operators of Talmud Torahs. The NCJE also launched *Jewish Education,* a professional journal.

The Shift to Synagogue Schools

As Jews moved from areas of first and second settlement, enrollment shifted toward synagogue-based schools. From 1910 to 1935, the number of children enrolled in synagogue-based Jewish schools rose from 35 percent to 60 percent. While Talmud Torah schools usually met four or five days, ten to twelve hours a week, congregational schools usually provided no more than six weekly hours of instruction, with Sunday school programs—typically sponsored by Reform congregations—offering only two or three hours of instruction.

In a notable resolution adopted in 1923, which only gradually came to reflect practice, the Commission on Jewish Education of the Union of American Hebrew Congregations urged that UAHC schools add a weekday session to the existing Sunday program, "in building up a system of religious education that will be adequate to our needs."[212] In 1913, Solomon Schechter had founded the United Synagogue of America—later renamed United Synagogue of Conservative Judaism—including a call for "the establishment of Jewish religious schools, in the curricula of which the study of the Hebrew language and literature shall be given a prominent place, both as the key to the true understanding of Judaism, and as a bond holding together the scattered communities of Israel throughout the world."[213] Nonetheless, the realities of congregational education in the 1920s and 1930s did not always mirror the aspirations of the elites who pronounced policy.

Zevi Scharfstein, a proponent of the communal Talmud Torah system and the author of many textbooks of the era, discusses the rise of the suburban congregational school in his *History of Jewish Education,* a mid-twentieth-century multivolume work in Hebrew:

> All the days of the week, there is no worshiper [in the modern suburban synagogue]—except in the *bais midrash,* where the elderly gather; likewise, on Shabbat, few are those who come. . . . Therefore, other uses are found for the synagogue: organizational meeting place, wedding and party hall, and school. The rabbi is, of course, the principal. . . . [The rabbi] worries most about training "worshipers" for the synagogue, and prayerbook reading becomes central. Similarly, there are rabbis who listen and acquiesce to parents who want to fulfill the obligation of Jewish education with two or three meetings per week. . . . The child studies in a Jewish school but leaves without real knowledge.[214]

Scharfstein's critique is anchored in the cultural Zionist orientation in which he was rooted. Synagogues were emerging as the primary centers of children's Jewish education, and preparation for participation in synagogue ritual was a curricular interest of sponsoring congregations. That instructional hours were reduced reflected—even among those affiliating with synagogues and sending their children to "Hebrew school"—an abiding interest for Americanization; daily blocks of time dedicated to Jewish learning were, for most families, out of the question. As to the hours that were dedicated to such study, there was no well-articulated vision of what represented "real (essential) knowledge."

Despite the decline of the communal, Hebraic Zionist–oriented Talmud Torah, the supplementary schools operated by congregations of the growing Conservative movement continued to emphasize Hebrew language—hence, the common appellation "Hebrew school." While Hebrew had, at one time, been seen as a means to accessing classical Jewish texts—"Talmud Torah" in its literal sense of "studying Torah"—Hebrew proficiency, both in communal and many Conservative congregational schools, increasingly occupied center stage. Over time, classical Hebrew texts came to be studied with an emphasis on improving Hebrew language skill rather than focusing primarily on the substance of the text.

Institutions of Rabbinic Learning

In addition to the earlier-established HUC, JTS, and RIETS, a number of centers of advanced Jewish learning were established in the early decades of the twentieth century, as Eastern European immigration continued. These included: Tifereth Yerushalayim of New York (1908); Torah V'daath of New York (1918); Hebrew Theological College of Chicago (1922); Ner Israel of Baltimore (1934); and the Jewish Institute of Religion, organized in New York in 1922 (JIR, founded by Stephen S. Wise, was to become part of HUC in 1950). JIR, a liberal rabbinical seminary, was—unlike HUC—pro-Zionist and wholeheartedly welcoming of the immigrant Eastern European Jews. Among the Orthodox yeshivot, the Hebrew Theological College, as the reorganized RIETS, looked to synthesize Orthodoxy and American life; the other new entries to the yeshiva world represented a strategy of resistance to the local environment, aimed at carrying forward the inherited culture of Eastern European traditionalism.

RIETS, which had been headed since 1915 by Lithuanian-born scholar Bernard Revel, opened the College of Arts and Sciences alongside its rabbinical school in 1928.[215] Revel had studied at the Yeshiva of Telz and, after emigrating, earned a doctorate at the recently established

Dropsie College—an independent academic institution in Philadelphia dedicated to graduate research in Jewish and related branches of learning. Revel aimed to "build a bridge over which the Torah could be brought from Europe to America and without compromise be made meaningful in contemporary American life."[216] In 1929, Revel recruited Rabbi Moses Soloveitchik, scion of a world-renowned rabbinic family, to head the RIETS faculty. On the death of Rabbi Soloveitchik in 1941, his son, Rabbi Joseph Soloveitchik, a Talmudic scholar with a doctorate from the University of Berlin, became head of the RIETS Talmud faculty. The "Rav," as Soloveitchik came to be known, was to emerge as a primary ideologue of American Orthodoxy in the 1940s and beyond.[217] At RIETS, intensive Talmud study was the major focus of rabbinic training. Revel reported to the yeshiva's board of directors that RIETS students devoted twenty-three hours a week to Talmud study.[218] Moreover, students tended to arrive at the school with substantial background in the study of such texts.

Kaufmann Kohler, who served as president of Hebrew Union College from 1903 to 1921, had considerable disdain for Talmudic dialectics. Kohler, whose religious ideology was expressed in the Pittsburgh Platform of 1885, also brooked no tolerance of Zionist leanings. Throughout his tenure, modern Hebrew was not taught at the college.[219] Bible, with emphasis on the Prophets, occupied center stage in the HUC curriculum during the Kohler years, with attention to philosophy, midrash, and history.[220] For Kohler, Zionism and Hebrew represented a retreat from universalism. Several faculty members resigned at the beginning of Kohler's presidency; indeed, the first to leave, in 1904, was Judah Magnes. Nonetheless, the college faculty expanded during Kohler's administration.

Despite Kohler's opposition toward Zionism, greater numbers of students—and graduates—were of Eastern European background and brought their affinity for Zionism to the institution and, in time, to the movement. By 1900, 48 percent of HUC students were children of Russian- or Polish-born parents.[221] Kohler was succeeded, in 1923, by Julian Morgenstern, an HUC alumnus and professor of Bible. During Morgenstern's presidency, scholarship flourished at the college; a dozen refugee European Jewish scholars found a haven at HUC, largely through his efforts.[222] Though Kaufmann Kohler's curricular program remained essentially in place, modern Hebrew and Zionism were permitted a voice at the college in the Morgenstern era.

At the Jewish Theological Seminary, Solomon Schechter was succeeded as president by Cyrus Adler, who served until his death in 1940.
Adler, an American-born semiticist who trained at Johns Hopkins University, took part in founding the Jewish Publication Society of America
in 1888. Adler was a founder of the American Jewish Historical Society
in 1892, served on the staff of the Smithsonian Institution, played a
leading role in the reorganization of the Seminary and its engagement of
Solomon Schechter, was president of Dropsie College, and edited numerous publications, including the first seven volumes of the *American
Jewish Year Book* and the *Jewish Quarterly Review* from 1916 to 1940.
Consistent with Adler's personal interests, it was during his tenure that
JTS developed a world-class library collection. During Adler's leadership, as under that of Schechter, the JTS curriculum dedicated nearly
half of students' instructional time to Talmud and Codes. Unlike HUC,
which embraced Higher Criticism, JTS avoided the matter of biblical
authorship.[223] Adler's successor was Louis Finkelstein, a JTS alumnus.
Both HUC and JTS had succeeded in educating leaders who could
carry forward the spiritual-religious mission articulated by these institutions' founders. When Bernard Revel died, in 1940, he was succeeded at
the Rabbi Isaac Elchanan Theological Seminary by Samuel Belkin.
Belkin, ordained at the Chafetz Chaim Yeshiva in Poland, had earned a
doctorate at Brown University and served at Yeshiva College as instructor in Greek and Hellenistic literature as well as on the RIETS Talmud
faculty.

Impact of the Depression

The impact of the Depression on Talmud Torah enrollment is reflected
in a period analysis of changing patterns of Jewish school attendance in
Cleveland in the mid-1930s. The researcher observed:

1. The [Talmud Torah] schools are situated in immigrant sections from
   which young parents are steadily moving away. No branches have
   been opened in the new Jewish neighborhoods. In fact some of the
   older branches had to be closed for lack of funds.
2. Those who remain in the immigrant sections are relatively the
   poorer element of the population. Forty percent of the children en-

rolled in the Hebrew schools are from relief families, the schools thus becoming "schools for the poor" and their social prestige has further been lowered.

3. As a result of the depression also, private schools have been opened in which unemployed persons—frequently ill-prepared—give instruction in *ivri* (mechanical Hebrew reading), *broches* (recitation of blessing) and bar mitzvah, at a pittance, and these schools compete with the Hebrew Schools. Some who were able to pay formerly, but now cannot, prefer to give their children "private instruction" rather than to accept what might be termed charity.[224]

Despite the Depression, there were new initiatives in Jewish education in the 1930s, a number of which were created by and for women. In 1934, Hadassah, launched earlier in the century by Henrietta Szold, created the School for the Jewish Woman in New York, offering afternoon and evening classes. Subsequently, Hadassah initiated the American Zionist Youth Commission, which sent speakers to chapters throughout the country, lecturing on Jewish history and tradition as well as on contemporary issues.[225] In 1935, the Women's League of the Conservative movement issued *The Adventures of K'tonton,* using the exploits of a Tom Thumb–like boy to examine Jewish rituals and festivals. This was followed by Althea O. Silverman's *Jewish Home Beautiful* in 1941.[226]

Other initiatives of the era were school-based. In 1937, the Ramaz School in Manhattan and the Maimonides School in Boston were established. These modern Orthodox coeducational day schools aimed to provide outstanding general education alongside education in classical Jewish texts, synthesizing Jewish learning and secular knowledge.[227] Rabbi Haskel Lookstein, a graduate of the first high school class of Ramaz, in 1949, went on to Columbia University and RIETS. The successor to his father, Joseph Lookstein, as rabbi of Kehilath Jeshurun and principal of Ramaz, he described the Ramaz ideal as a fusion of "two traditions within one wholesome, integrated respectful and dignified young man [read: person on] whom the Jewish and non-Jewish world would look with pride and admiration and say 'here is a product of a yeshiva education.'"[228] This worldview was different from that of most yeshivot, which tended to view general education in utilitarian terms and rejected "synthesis" as an ideal.

In 1939, the establishment of the Beth Hayeled—"House of the Child"—School in New York signified an experiment in Jewish preschool education. Children entered the program at the age of three, remained at Beth Hayeled for five years, and transferred to public school and a neighborhood Talmud Torah in the third grade. Soon after this program began, other early childhood foundation schools were established.[229] This mirrored a trend in public education to view and structure kindergarten through third grade as a distinctive unit with a continuous developmental sequence.[230]

Curricularizing Ideology

Mordecai Kaplan's epic Reconstructionist manifesto, *Judaism as a Civilization* (1934), gave expression to ideas that Kaplan—long active in Jewish educational initiatives—had advanced for decades. Kaplan, who influenced generations of rabbis and Jewish educators through his teaching at the Jewish Theological Seminary and later, through the institutionalization of his teachings at the Reconstructionist Rabbinical College, stated:

> Jews must abandon the notion that the Jewish school, or the class for adults, is the primary conveyor of Jewish education. The mistake of limiting education to formal instruction is the primary cause of the complete failure and breakdown of Jewish educational endeavor. Were the school to be regarded as the only means of transmitting Judaism to the rising generation, Jews would have to follow the example of the Catholics and establish a parochial school system of Jewish education. Yet if the public school system, despite the unlimited financial resources, falls far short of some of its primary purposes, what could the Jews hope to accomplish with their limited resources, were they to be responsible for the entire education of the child? And even if such segregation of Jewish children were feasible, it is scarcely desirable. . . . Even with highly trained teachers and ideal facilities, there is no possibility of attaining any of the objectives of Jewish education, if Jewish education is to be limited to the training given the child in the religious or Hebrew school.[231]

For Kaplan, every aspect of Jewish life—its social welfare activities, support for the upbuilding of Palestine, and all collective efforts—needed to be purposively educative. Yet, however intensive and extensive the ongoing Jewish educational input might be, Kaplan opined, "the Jew in America will be first and foremost an American, and only secondarily a Jew."[232]

Kaplan, who headed the Seminary's Teachers Institute from 1909 to 1946, and Benderly, who led the New York BJE from 1910 to 1941, and their students saw the critical challenge of the generation as balancing Jewish survival and integration as Americans. Jewish peoplehood and Jewish unity were essential pillars of this agenda. Consistent with this approach, textbooks of the era emphasized the fundamental congruence of American and Jewish values.[233] There was also a toning down of the demonization of Christianity, a definition of the Jews as a people and not merely a religious group, and a promotion of cultural Zionism coupled with an affirmation of faith in the United States as hospitable to Jews.[234]

In 1923, Emanuel Gamoran, a protégé of Benderly and Kaplan, assumed the newly established position of educational director of the Reform movement's Commission on Jewish Education, a joint venture between the Central Conference of American Rabbis and the Union of American Hebrew Congregations. Gamoran held this position until 1958. His aim was to reinfuse peoplehood—a concept abandoned by nineteenth-century Reform—into Reform Jewish education.

Gamoran—a Zionist who, after returning with his wife from a nine-month trip to Palestine in 1924, continued to speak Hebrew at home—encouraged the Union to move away from Sunday school moralizing and toward concrete activities. He did not repudiate Reform ideology; rather, he presented his agenda as a didactic approach. Through "purposeful activities," he explained, "the child will form useful habits—he will develop his character because he will have learned to make proper responses to various situations."[235] Consistent with this view, Gamoran's curricular program gave primacy to Jewish customs and ceremonies over ethics, and Jewish songs and Jewish current events over catechisms. Reflecting their own sense of Jewish peoplehood, the Gamorans maintained a kosher household so that all Jews would be able to eat there.

One of the earliest UAHC textbook publications during Gamoran's tenure was Lee Levinger's *A History of the Jews in the United States*.[236] Levinger tried to explain the differences between the three Jewish religious movements. After describing each stream, its institutions, and leaders, Levinger emphasizes the unity of all Jews:

But everyone knows that the differences between synagogues are comparatively trivial; what is most important is that they are all places where Jews worship God. All rabbis are preachers and teachers of Judaism. All rabbinical seminaries teach their students the Bible, the Talmud, Jewish history, Jewish philosophy of the Middle Ages, the same necessary subjects which a Jewish leader must know. All Jews agree in their main ideas about God and man. No Jews agree with Christians in these same points, or in most of them.[237]

Though acknowledging the variety of Jewish religious expressions, the author's conclusion is that the Jews are fundamentally united—and collectively distinguishable in belief from Christians. The vision or ideal that rendered Judaism its enduring significance was not, however, addressed. Another significant publication of the Gamoran era was *Hillel's Happy Holidays*, by Gamoran's wife, Mamie. The book, publication of which was made possible by the Reform movement's National Federation of Temple Sisterhoods, was designed to teach Jewish holidays and customs. Readers followed the life of Hillel, a schoolchild, over the course of a yearly cycle of Jewish holidays and were thereby introduced to a rich array of practices. As Gamoran noted in his introduction to his wife's work: "It is [an] object of this book to provide the kind of material which will acquaint Jewish children not only with those customs and ceremonies which they may themselves practice at home or in the synagogue, but also to develop on their part a sympathetic attitude to the customs observed by other Jews."[238] Consistent with the social norms of the interwar period, Hillel, in Mamie Gamoran's book, only interacts with *Jews* of diverse backgrounds. The publications launched by Emanuel Gamoran bridged the gap between Eastern European and German Jews. Given Gamoran's broad view and the fact that the UAHC was the only national organization printing such texts expressly for use in schools, these publications found their way into Conservative and Orthodox schools.[239] Gamoran's approach was, over decades, to become pervasive in Reform Jewish education.

By the beginning of World War II, 7,000 students were attending thirty day schools—90 percent of which were in New York—but most Orthodox leaders shared the view that, when it came to formal Jewish schooling, the congregationally sponsored Talmud Torah was to be the primary institutional framework for Jewish education in the United

States. In 1942, the Union of Orthodox Jewish Congregations (UOJC) published a curriculum guide for Talmud Torah education. The curriculum, which its authors indicated "has been successfully realized in several Talmud Torahs in this country," was ideally designed for a ten-hour-a-week school.[240] In like manner to the educational programs developed and promoted by Samson Benderly, the Orthodox "Model Program" called for *ivrit b'ivrit,* Hebrew-based, instruction: "The language of instruction for all subjects in this program is Hebrew, this being the language of the Holy Scriptures and of Eretz Israel. It is the language of Jews throughout the world."[241] Though influenced by the pedagogic approach of the Benderly school, the UOJC manual made it clear that it rejected any deviation from traditional Jewish belief and practice: "Any tendency of Judaism that would abridge the scope of divine Torah is a retrogression to heathenism, and any (reconstruction) that runs counter to the spirit and the letter of Jewish tradition is destruction."[242]

Despite the creative efforts of the generation, the overarching question remained: "Jewish education, for what?" The *hadarim,* along with the Hebraic, cultural Zionist Talmud Torahs of the second and third decades of the nineteenth century, were being supplanted by congregational afternoon schools. Was Judaism to be taught in the synagogue school as religion or as peoplehood? As particular or as universal? Through its Hebrew sources or in translation? Though the Conservative movement's Commission on Jewish Education of the United Synagogue, established in 1940, urged an educational program of no fewer than six hours a week, what vision of the educated Jew underlay the hours standard?

Early Impact of Holocaust-Era Refugees

With the relocation of several leading personalities of Jewish educational life from Europe to the United States before and during World War II, a number of new institutions appeared on the American scene, each of which was to have considerable impact in the ensuing decades. These institutional developments included the establishment of Lubavitcher (Hasidic) schools with the arrival of the Lubavitcher rebbe in 1940; the creation of Beth Jacob (Bais Yaakov) girls' schools, modeled on a network of such traditionalist schools established in Poland in the early 1940s; and the founding of the Telshe Yeshiva in Cleveland (1941) and of the Beth Medrash Govoha in Lakewood, New Jersey (1943). In 1944, under the direction of Shraga Feivel Mendlowitz, an immigrant from Austria-Hungary who had studied with noted European rabbinic scholars and had significantly expanded Brooklyn's Torah V'daath yeshiva, an ambitious, national Orthodox day school initiative was launched.

Mendlowitz, who had devoted himself to Jewish education since arriving in the United States in 1913, wanted to reinvigorate and unite a national network of yeshiva day schools. Toward that end, he enlisted Samuel Feuerstein, a successful business executive, to serve as president of the Torah Umesorah Society for the Establishment of Torah Schools. The articles of incorporation of the organization established the ideological authority of a body of Orthodox rabbis in all matters of religious life:

> There shall be an ecclesiastical governing body, to be known as the Rabbinical Supervisory Council, consisting of fifteen duly ordained Rabbis of Orthodox Hebrew Faith, who shall have supervisory control and direction of all matters concerning and relating to (a) religious problems and questions, and to (b) the religious functions, purposes and objects of the corporation— and such other powers not in derogation of those specifically provided herein as may be provided by the By-Laws. All acts of the trustees in their administration of the affairs of the corporation, and to revenues, insofar as such acts concern or relate to (a) any matter constituting, affecting or bearing upon any religious problem or question, or to (b) religious functions, purposes or objects of the corporation shall be subject to the discipline, rules, usages, control and approval of said Rabbinical Supervisory Council, to which this corporation is hereby declared subject. The Rabbinical Supervisory Council shall have sole right to determine what act involves a matter constituting, affecting or bearing upon any religious problem or question, or the religious functions, purposes or objects of the corporation.[243]

Thus, on American soil, a traditionalist rabbinic panel was established as the halakhic authority of a system of Orthodox day schools to be established. The Rabbinical Supervisory Council would determine the very scope of its jurisdiction since it would decide what was a religious matter. A group of Orthodox rabbinical leaders was constituted, and Torah Umesorah launched into the establishment of hundreds of Jewish day schools nationwide. In the 1940s, ninety-seven Jewish day schools were founded in the United States and Canada, many of them nurtured by Torah Umesorah. Such schools often reflected the needs and aspirations of Holocaust-era refugees. But not all Orthodox day schools turned for guidance to Torah Umesorah. Such groups as United Lubavitcher Yeshivoth (and, later, other Hasidic groups transplanted to America because of the Holocaust), the National Council for Torah Education (of the Religious Zionists of America), and the National Council of Beth Jacob Schools were among those promoting particular types of day school education for Jews in the U.S. by the end of World War II.

The period 1910–45 saw extraordinary institutional development in Jewish education. Beyond any single aspect of Jewish education, however, was a shift in communal perspective as to the locus of responsibility for providing Jewish education to successive generations. Jewish Federations saw Jewish education as part of the communal agenda and, typically, established Bureaus of Jewish Education to address this domain. From early childhood to the college campus and beyond, diverse settings and structures of Jewish education were initiated.

At the close of World War II, American Jewry stood at the threshold of a generation of tremendous growth. New suburban communities, a baby boom, news of Palestine/Israel, unprecedented educational opportunities through the G.I. Bill for war veterans, a religious revival, heightened interest in adult education, tremendous growth in camping, and interfaith dialogue were transformative. And, as the public became fully aware of the devastation of the Holocaust, it was apparent that the world had changed.

CHAPTER FIVE
Jewish Education in a World Transformed, 1945–75

The dominant motifs of American Jewish life from 1945 to 1975 were suburbanization and synagogue growth; and one of the chief functions of the synagogue as understood at mid-century was the provision of Jewish education. At least a billion dollars was spent on a thousand new synagogue buildings in the 1950s and 1960s.[244] Many of the young families in new suburban areas had not previously been involved in congregational activity. The synagogue represented an expression of Jewish group feeling and was seen as a primary vehicle, particularly with the decline of Jewish neighborhoods, for Jewish education and socialization of the younger generation. Religion was an accepted means of retaining group identity; thus, American Jews could comfortably identify with Judaism as one of the three great faiths, alongside Protestantism and Catholicism. As the westward movement of Jews continued—with Los Angeles Jewry growing from 160,000 to 480,000 inhabitants between 1945 and 1965—the Jewish Theological Seminary and Hebrew Union College established West Coast branches in Los Angeles, in 1947 and 1954, respectively.

The Union of American Hebrew Congregations grew from 334 congregations in 1948 to 664 in 1966, while the United Synagogue grew from 350 affiliates at the close of World War II to 800 by 1965.[245] In the post–World War II generation, Conservative affiliation rose most dramatically. For suburban, one-synagogue communities, the Conservative movement represented centrism. For the substantial population of returning military personnel, Conservative-style worship was familiar from their recent overseas experience, because U.S. military chaplains tended to conduct religious services along middle-of-the-road, Conservative lines.[246] For American-born children of Eastern European immi-

79

grants, the Conservative stream, unlike Reform, represented a measure of continuity with traditionalism, and it was clearly more in step with American ways than the Orthodox ritual. The movement's emphasis on community was appealing to those for whom suburban synagogue membership substituted for the Jewish neighborhood of the previous generation. By functioning as a synagogue center, "suburban Conservative synagogues helped to diminish the loneliness of transplanted urban Jews living on the suburban frontier. They provided a communal setting for Jews who shared common generational experiences, as well as the trials and tribulations of geographic and socioeconomic mobility in postwar America."[247]

In the 1950s, the Conservative movement permitted driving to the synagogue on Shabbat and calling women to the Torah for *aliyot*, which validated the notion that, however conservative it might be, the movement was accepting of American realities and norms. Orthodoxy in America seemed to be in decline in the 1950s, but by the 1970s—reenergized by Orthodox refugees and a flourishing day school movement—it was growing institutionally and in the intensity of learning and commitment of its adherents to ritual practice. In the 1950s and 1960s, the rate of synagogue affiliation climbed from the 20 percent of the 1930s to nearly 60 percent.[248] Church attendance was high, and American society validated Sunday school attendance as an expression of wholesome, middle-class values. Though the number of students in Jewish educational settings reached unprecedented highs in the 1960s, the underlying question, "Jewish distinctiveness—for what purpose?" remained largely unaddressed. By the mid-1970s, the very prospect of Jewish survival in the United States was much discussed.

After World War II, some 140,000 Holocaust survivors came to the United States, joining the more than 200,000 refugees who had been admitted between 1933 and 1945. Among the most recent arrivals were Jews from very traditional Jewish societies, who served as a cultural booster shot, demanding more intensive Jewish education. As one rabbi noted: "Post-Holocaust parents were not satisfied with the quality of Jewish education that they found when they came here. They came from the land of the *gedolim* [great rabbinic authorities]."[249] Awareness of the destruction of most European Jewry left many American Jews with a sense of responsibility to affirm Jewish identification. The founding of the State of Israel engendered pride in Jewish identification for many people, and the establishment of the Jewish state gave renewed significance to the teaching of modern Hebrew in Jewish schools.[250]

Growth of Congregational Schools

The post–World War II baby boom, combined with escalating rates of synagogue membership and Jewish school attendance, resulted in a near-tripling of students enrolled in Jewish schools, from 200,000 in 1937 to 589,000 in 1962. By 1962, 92 percent of students enrolled in Jewish schools studied under synagogue auspices.[251] Yiddish schools, which, at their peak, had served over 5 percent of the Jewish school population, enrolled less than 2 percent by the late 1950s, as Yiddish culture declined with the passing of the immigrant generation.[252] In the 1930s, only 10,000 students—5 percent of total enrollment—were enrolled in high school programs of Jewish education; by 1959, closer to 10 percent of the expanded population of students was to be found in Jewish secondary schools.[253] For those who, early in the twenty-first century, bemoan low levels of Jewish educational participation at the high school level, it is noteworthy that over the decades there has been a gradual escalation in the percentage of students of this cohort enrolled in Jewish educational institutions.[254]

Conservative movement leadership urged a program of six hours a week—typically spread over three sessions—to include Hebrew, Bible, prayer book, history, religion (customs and ceremonies), current events, and songs.[255] Schools were advised to conduct high school departments and to educate their students at least until age sixteen, lest the impact of elementary study be diminished. To promote this agenda, it was mandatory for bar and bat mitzvah candidates to enroll in a minimum of three years' instruction in a six-hour-a-week—spread over three weekly meetings—congregational school, and confirmation was to require at least five years' enrollment and a minimum age of fifteen.[256]

The public bat mitzvah ceremony, introduced by Mordecai Kaplan in the 1920s, became widespread in Conservative congregations in the 1950s and 1960s. By 1959, 74 percent of Conservative congregations met the six-hour weekly instructional standard.[257] With boys and girls jointly experiencing an identical course of study in an increasingly egalitarian society, with one aim of Hebrew school being preparation for synagogue worship and with congregational school participation defining eligibility for a bar or bat mitzvah, more families embraced a synagogue bat mitzvah ceremony as a rite of passage for daughters. Though the age of bat mitzvah is traditionally twelve (rather than the thirteen for bar mitzvah)—reflecting the earlier physical maturation of adolescent girls—the standard, egalitarian curriculum for boys and girls gave rise to the convention of bat mitzvah as well as bar mitzvah ceremonies being held soon after the student turned thirteen. The Reform movement, too, tried to "raise the bar." Commenting on the state of Reform congregational education in 1946, Emanuel Gamoran observed that owing to a generation of "propaganda" on behalf of weekday instruction, 25 percent of Reform religious schools had introduced weekday, in addition to Sunday, sessions. Instruction included holidays, biblical and postbiblical heroes, Jewish history and literature, Bible selections, prayers, Hebrew, singing, current events and modern Jewish problems, and the Jewish contribution to civilization.[258]

Isa Aron notes that the 1950s and 1960s represented the heyday of congregational schooling, owing to a constellation of factors: "The newness and excitement of the State of Israel validated the teaching of modern Hebrew. A cadre of American-born teachers, mostly women, existed. . . . Because day schools were still a relatively new phenomenon, congregational schools retained a core of committed, knowledgeable parents. The rates of intermarriage and divorce were lower, as were the number of 'working mothers.'"[259] During these decades, the Sephardic pronunciation of Hebrew, which had become the spoken dialect of Israel, became prevalent in American Jewish education (paradoxically, in all but the most Orthodox and Reform circles).

Day School Growth

In 1944, Alexander Dushkin, perhaps the most highly respected American Jewish educator of mid-century, observed: "At present, after sixty years of Yeshiva development, about 1 percent of our 700,000 children of elementary school age in the United States attend Jewish complete day schools; 99 percent attend the public schools. Even if such [day] schools increase tenfold in the course of years, 90 percent of our children would still be in public schools."[260] Jewish day schools, which had been rare before 1940, rapidly proliferated after World War II, often spearheaded by Orthodox refugees who had found asylum in the United States. Within a generation, the tenfold increase that Dushkin had anticipated as so remote a possibility had been realized.

The Torah Umesorah school network grew from ninety-five schools with 14,000 students in 1946 to 330 schools with 67,000 students in the early 1970s.[261] By 1975, there were 425 Orthodox day schools, including 138 high schools, with a total enrollment of 82,200.[262] The ideological orientation of the traditional, yeshiva wing of the Torah Umesorah day school movement was expressed by Rabbi Mordecai Gifter of the Telshe Yeshiva in Cleveland: "The function of Torah *chinuch* [education] is the creation of a society where Torah will not merely be one of a vast number of human interests but rather a society where all human interest, all human endeavor, centers in and emanates from Torah. The proper function of Torah *chinuch,* therefore, is the development of an understanding and an appreciation of the nature of Torah and *Mitzvos.*"[263] Inherent in Torah education is the concept of *amal Hatorah,* "labor in the Torah." Rabbi Gifter explained that "*amal Hatorah* means the complete engrossment of the student in Torah to the exclusion of all else. It means a mind completely open to Torah, unburdened by other systems of thought."[264] Some leaders of the traditional yeshiva world sought to re-create the lost institutions of Eastern Europe on American soil. Rabbi Joel Teitelbaum, the Satmar rebbe, who arrived in New York from Hungary by way of Jerusalem in 1946, established a staunchly antimodernist, anti-Zionist Hasidic enclave—complete with its own educational institutions—in Brooklyn. A generation later, this community developed an independent village, Kiryas Joel—named for its rebbe—in Monroe Township, in Orange County, New York.[265] Neither the Lubavitch circle, which had its own educational infrastructure, nor the antimodernist Hasidic groups looked to Torah Umesorah for guidance or networking.

The traditional yeshiva view differed from what Rabbi Joseph Lookstein, director of the Ramaz School and professor of homiletics at Yeshiva University, termed the "integrated yeshiva" approach. Rather than insulating the child against the environment, "[t]he objective of the Integrated Yeshiva is to integrate American and Hebraic cultures, or to achieve a blending of Judaism and Americanism."[266] This approach, in the parlance of the time, aimed at synthesis. Over time, proponents of the integrated yeshiva found their aims no longer aligned with Torah Umesorah, which—as Orthodoxy enjoyed a resurgence—became less accepting of positions that its rabbinical council had tolerated early in the development of day schools. The tension within Orthodoxy between resistance and accommodation to American norms remains a continuing theme.

Half of the school day in Torah Umesorah schools was usually devoted to Torah studies and the other half to general education. Consistent with the aforementioned diversity in outlook, variations in the apportionment of time between Torah studies and general studies, the language of religious studies instruction (English, Hebrew, or Yiddish), the choice of texts within the classical religious literature, and structure of the school day were wide-ranging. In Hasidic schools and the most traditional yeshivot, thirty to forty hours a week might be dedicated to Jewish studies and ten to fifteen hours to general education.

From the 1940s to the 1960s, significant numbers of Torah studies educators in day schools were European immigrants. As Orthodox rabbinical seminaries grew and yeshiva day school enrollment increased, American-educated teachers—themselves yeshiva graduates—became commonplace. Those yeshiva graduates who became teachers tended to be graduates of the more traditional yeshivot. Those whose ideology was one of synthesis opted, by and large, for other professional pursuits. In the 1960s, the great majority of day schools were under Orthodox sponsorship, but about a third of the students enrolled in yeshiva day schools came from homes that were not Orthodox.[267]

The establishment of a Reform Jewish day school was first raised publicly in 1950 by Emanuel Gamoran. He addressed a convention of Reform rabbis:

> Surely there is no reason why day schools in America should be represented only by the non-Liberal elements on the American Jewish scene. Certainly there ought to be a place to which a liberal Jew, lay or rabbinic, who wishes his child to get an intensive Jewish education may be able to send him without exposing him to indoctrination with an Orthodox ideology. . . . We must face the facts frankly and seek, under our own auspices and in certain favorable situations, to establish day schools for perhaps 10 percent of our pupils that will meet our needs. There is no reason why such private day schools should not be able to hold their own with the best private day schools in the country, or why in addition to the general education that the children would receive, they should not also have an intensive Jewish education with a good Hebraic base, in which Jewish and general instruction would be so integrated that the personality developed would be a unified, intelligent, Liberal American Jew.[268]

Gamoran argued that there was no good reason for day schools to be under the exclusive sponsorship of Orthodox providers. At mid-twentieth century, however, confidence in public schools was high, and day school education flew in the face of the ideal of public education that Isaac Mayer Wise had articulated and that had been broadly embraced eighty years earlier. Two decades and considerable societal change were to elapse before action on Gamoran's proposal was to be taken within Reform institutions.

While Gamoran's remarks were, in the near term, ignored by the Reform movement, a number of Conservative congregations launched day schools under synagogue sponsorship. In 1946, Congregation Anshe Emet in Chicago opened a community day school, and in 1950, Temple Beth El in New York created a Conservative day school. By 1958, fourteen Conservative day schools were in operation.[269]

In 1958, the United Synagogue Commission on Jewish Education urged Conservative congregations, singly or cooperatively, to establish day schools. It noted that "while the congregational supplementary religious school will continue as the basic educational agency for a large majority of our children, it is certain that the day school can offer far superior facilities for instruction in the Hebrew language, Bible, Talmud, and medieval and modern Hebrew literature. . . . The growth of the day school will help the Conservative movement to create a reservoir of intensively educated and deeply dedicated men and women from whom the American Jewish community can draw professional and lay leadership."[270] Several additional Conservative day schools were founded in the late 1950s and 1960s; in 1964, the Solomon Schechter Day School Association was formed, linking Conservative Jewish day schools. By 1977, nearly 10,000 students were enrolled in fifty Solomon Schechter schools.[271]

Among the conditions that made such growth possible were economic prosperity and a sense of security as Americans. No longer did a Jew need to attend public school to become Americanized. Busing to achieve racial desegregation in public schools, a perceived erosion of values, and the declining effectiveness of public education contributed to non-Orthodox parents' readiness to consider Jewish day school.[272] As many Orthodox day schools gradually became more stridently committed to traditionalism, existing Jewish day school options became less comfortable for liberal Jews. Sociologist Samuel Heilman explains the shift to the right in Orthodox educational settings as an expression of estrangement from American cultural trends of the time: "By the end of the 1970s, in the wake of racial turmoil, after violent Vietnam War protests, growing radicalism on campus, polarization in the political process, the excesses of the sexual revolution, freethinking in lifestyle choices, and increasing signs of a decline in Jewish affiliation and involvement among young college graduates, the American dream seemed to growing numbers of Orthodox Jews to have become a nightmare."[273] Thus some of the same social concerns that encouraged the interest of non-Orthodox Jewish families in considering Jewish day school education fostered what Heilman terms a "slide to the right" in many of the Orthodox-sponsored schools that had previously been more culturally aligned with the aspirations of non-Orthodox Jewish populations.

In the Reform movement, a petition signed by fifty students and faculty of HUC-JIR in New York in 1961 called upon the Commission on Jewish Education to investigate the establishment of day schools. The petitioners declared: "We, the undersigned, believe that the need for a more complete Jewish education, at present, warrants our urgent attention. So too, we believe, it warrants the Commission's reconsideration and reevaluation of the establishment of Liberal-Jewish Day Schools as one of the better possible solutions to that problem."[274] At the HUC Founders Day Ceremony in 1968, HUC professor Stanley Chyet argued that inasmuch as Judaism is a way of life, it requires daily experience by way of educational process; hence, the rationale for day schools was compelling.[275] Notwithstanding voices within the movement calling for a day school initiative, at the 1969 Reform convention a resolution to establish "pilot programs and experimental projects in full-time Reform Jewish education" was narrowly defeated.

Nonetheless, in 1970, two Reform temples—Congregation Rodeph Sholom in New York and Temple Beth Am in Miami—opened day schools. The emergence of Reform day schools represented a coalescence of parental concern for quality secular education and the interest of rabbinic leadership in quality Jewish education. Of great significance was the fact that private schooling was undergoing democratization in the eyes of Reform Jews. While private schooling had at one time been the domain of the northeast elites and Catholics, there had been a broadening of the pool of private school students under the impact of court-ordered busing and a perceived decline in the quality of public education, as well as a dramatic decrease in Catholic school enrollment. Private schools had, in turn, become far more diverse than in previous generations.[276]

Beth Am's Rabbi Herbert Baumgard envisioned a religious studies program representing one-sixth to one-fifth of the total curriculum and emphasizing "Judaism as the celebration of life." The vision of Rodeph

Sholom was articulated in universalistic terms as aiming "to develop character values and ethical ideals leading to responsible citizenship" and was "open to all pupils who can qualify for its academic requirements, regardless of faiths or origins."[277] By 1981, there were nine Reform day schools. Not until 1985, however, were day schools formally approved by the Union of American Hebrew Congregations. In 1990, a Reform day school network—Progressive Association of Reform Day Schools (PARDeS)—was established.

The foundation schools of the 1940s for students aged three through eight, combining Jewish and general education, were, on the one hand, being supplanted by day schools; on the other hand, early childhood, "nursery" centers for preschool children, which had expanded significantly during and after World War II—assuming an essential child-care role—continued to grow, not only under the auspices of Jewish Community Centers but at synagogues and, in some cases, at elementary day schools. This mirrored American trends in education, which saw early education as an opportunity for group socialization and character development. In 1900, only 7 percent of American five-year-olds attended kindergarten; by 1950, this figure had risen to 38 percent and by 1970 had reached 60 percent.[278]

Curriculum and Instruction

In 1959, the American Association for Jewish Education published the *Report of the Commission for the Study of Jewish Education in the United States,* based on an extensive survey. The report estimated that 40–45 percent of Jewish children aged five to fourteen were receiving Jewish schooling that year—though upward of 80 percent were enrolled at some time during their elementary school years. It pegged the average stay at three to four years.[279]

The report distinguished between Sunday school, weekday supplementary school, and day school faculties. Among day school faculty members, 69 percent were men and 31 percent women; 62 percent of those teachers were foreign-born. Among weekday Hebrew school teachers, 64 percent were men and 36 percent women; 61 percent were foreign-born. Among Sunday school teachers, 36 percent were men and 64 percent women; 89 percent were born in the United States.[280] The report noted that of the pool of Sunday school teachers, 58 percent claimed nothing beyond elementary Jewish education, and 9 percent claimed no Jewish education. Thus, "the general ignorance of Jewish religious culture on the part of our Sunday School teachers is here given statistical confirmation."[281] At the time of greatest growth in the number of schools, synagogues, and students, there was a dearth of personnel to meet the need. Not only were the various teachers' colleges unable to turn out sufficient graduates to meet rapidly escalating need; other professional opportunities after World War II far exceeded the standing of a career in Jewish education in income and status.

The Conservative movement had established the Jewish Educators Assembly in 1950, followed by the Reform movement's National Association of Temple Educators in 1954, but in 1969 Walter Ackerman, a close observer of the field, commented: "[T]here is a serious shortage of qualified personnel in Jewish education. . . . The idea of a profession of Jewish teacher is either a thing of the past or a hope for the future."[282] Ackerman was no less harsh in assessing educational achievement in congregational schools: "When judged by even the least demanding standard of what it means to be an educated Jew, it is hard to avoid the feeling that the academic aspirations of the one-day-a-week school are either a joke or an act of cynical pretentiousness. The plethora of subject matter of its curriculum is certainly beyond treatment in the available time, and even the most serious and able student cannot hope to acquire more than a smattering of information. . . . The three-day-a-week school of the Conservative movement cannot claim happier results."[283] Of those students who were enrolled in any type of Jewish school in any given year, the sorts of schools referenced by Ackerman were the schools that the overwhelming majority attended.

The sense that all was not right with congregational education led to curricular initiatives in the 1960s and 1970s. The Melton Research Center for Jewish Education at the Jewish Theological Seminary, funded by philanthropist Samuel Melton in order to improve supplementary Jewish education, brought together outstanding thinkers from the fields of general education, Jewish studies, and Jewish education, with the aim of "translating Jewish tradition into curriculum." This curriculum was to comprise Bible, Jewish thought, Jewish history, and ritual and was to foster Hebrew proficiency for literacy in Torah and siddur. It also aimed to nurture identity through affective learning.[284] During the same period, the Union of American Hebrew Congregations and United Synagogue each developed new curricular materials, and Behrman House

Publishers produced new textbooks that were successfully marketed to Conservative and Reform congregational schools. Trends in public education such as values clarification, cooperative learning, programmed instruction, and audiovisual technology also made their way into congregational schools in these years.[285]

Not long before Emanuel Gamoran's retirement as head of the Reform movement's Commission on Jewish Education, Central Conference of American Rabbis president Barnett Brickner signaled an impending shift in the movement's educational priorities. In his message to the 1955 CCAR Convention, Rabbi Brickner stated:

> Our Reform Jewish education has gone through several phases. At first it was largely Bible centered. . . . Then followed the second phase, when we realized that there is no necessary transfer from memorization to character formation; and we came to believe that knowledge is power—that, if we imparted more information about Israel, Zionism, Jewish history, the Hebrew language and literature, customs, ceremonies, etc., this would inevitably lead to the making of good Jews. During this phase there was an overemphasis on "peoplehood" and subject matter. We are now in the third phase, where we realize that the American child must be conditioned to become a reverent and believing Jew . . . one who feels spiritually secure in America.[286]

More personal religious ethics, greater openness to ritualism, and an emphasis on programs of social action—strongly encouraged by Rabbi Maurice Eisendrath, who led the Union of American Hebrew Congregations from 1943 to 1973—were among the trends in Reform Jewish education.

Walter Ackerman observed that a similar shift in emphasis can be seen in comparing the United Synagogue curriculum of 1922 with that of 1959. The 1922 curriculum strove "to create within the child a sense of exultation in those experiences of his people which have constituted for the race the very footprints of God"; the 1959 curriculum aspired "to imbue the child with love of God and trust in His Goodness." The first statement emphasized the collectivity, and the second postulated a more personal deity.[287]

A noteworthy addition to the changing curricula of the 1960s was the study of comparative religion. The National Conference of Christians and Jews had been established in 1928, and the interfaith goodwill movement gained strength after World War II. In 1955, Will Herberg published his classic *Protestant, Catholic, Jew.* Within a few years, the Union of American Hebrew Congregations published *Our Religion and Our Neighbors,* and Behrman House published *Judaism and Christianity: What We Believe.* Students who mastered the information in these texts could recognize similarities and differences between Jewish and Christian beliefs about God, human nature, sin, and salvation. They would also learn about various life-cycle events, calendars, and liturgies. These textbooks encouraged readers to view themselves as no different from their neighbors in values and citizenship, while maintaining religious boundaries between Jews and Christians; the religious sphere was narrowly circumscribed.[288]

Kolel (Inward) and Chabad (Outreach) Initiatives

The impact of Holocaust refugees on American Jewry included two phenomena introduced by notable rabbinic personalities who emigrated to America in the early 1940s. One, with a primarily inward focus, was the *kolel,* a full-time program of advanced Talmudic study for adult men of outstanding scholarly ability who are supported by stipends. The other, *kiruv*—"drawing near"—aimed to reach out to "lost" Jews.

The *kolel* was first introduced in America by Rabbi Aaron Kotler, a noted Talmudic scholar from Europe. He opened the *kolel* at the Beth Medrash Govoha in Lakewood, New Jersey, in 1943, with twelve graduates of American rabbinical schools. In 1945, fifteen men who had been Rabbi Kotler's students in Europe joined him at what came to be known as the Lakewood Kolel.[289]

A second *kolel,* Beth Medrash Elyon of Monsey—an extension of the Brooklyn-based Torah V'daath—was soon launched.[290] Whereas in 1950 there were no more than a hundred persons studying in American *kolellim* (plural of *kolel*), by the end of the 1970s the number of *kolel* participants exceeded 1,000.[291] A cultural transformation also occurred over the course of a generation; the *kolel* was democratized, no longer being exclusively for the most outstanding, elite students. This trend was to continue, resulting in substantial growth in *kolel* participation in the decades to follow. Toward the end of the twentieth century, a number of community *kolellim* were to direct their attention outward, actively seeking to engage in Torah study with people well outside the ambit of the traditional *kolel.*

The Chabad-Lubavitch movement, whose leadership was transplanted to the United States in the early 1940s, took an activist outreach approach early on. Lubavitcher rebbe Joseph I. Schneersohn sent two young disciples, Shlomo Carlebach and Zalman Schachter, to promote Jewish life among Jewish students on college campuses in 1949.[292] The subsequent careers of these outreach workers is testimony to the reciprocal influences of people and their environments. Carlebach was to develop his own following as a charismatic folk-singing rabbi—whose melodies were part of all Jewish religious movements—and Schachter was to become the patriarchal figure of a spiritual Jewish renewal movement. Beyond these two erstwhile college outreach workers, Chabad dispatched emissaries to many American communities in the post–World War II generation, in an effort to promote Jewish consciousness and practice. This outreach work was significantly expanded under the leadership of the seventh Lubavitcher rebbe, Menachem Mendel Schneersohn, who became head of the movement in 1951.

Nonformal Jewish Education

In the 1940s and early 1950s, Jewish residential summer camping fully blossomed as an educational enterprise. Sponsored by philanthropic societies, Jewish residential camps in the years before World War I provided relief from tenement conditions and taught immigrant children American ways. Camping as a Jewish educational vehicle had been piloted at Camp Cejwin by Albert Schoolman in 1919. Schoolman, principal of the Central Jewish Institute in New York, an institution much influenced by the thinking of Mordecai Kaplan, saw the camp as a vehicle for providing experiences in Jewish living and as a setting that could serve as a training ground for young adults entering careers in Jewish education and social service. As noted earlier, the Schoolmans, Berksons, and Dushkins established Camp Modin on a private basis, modeling it on Cejwin but appealing to a wealthier clientele.

In the 1920s and 1930s, several Yiddish and Zionist camp programs were launched, including camping initiatives by such Zionist youth movements as Hashomer Hatza'ir, Habonim, Young Judaea, and B'nei Akiva—then known as Hashomer Hadati.[293] The first Hebrew-speaking camp, Camp Achvah, was established by Samson Benderly in 1927.[294] Though it provided a rich educational experience, its early promise was cut short by the Depression.

In 1941, Camp Massad, a more enduring Hebrew-based Zionist camp, began operation. It was led for many years by founding director Shlomo Shulsinger, committed to the notion that "the Hebrew movement must serve as the foundation and the guide for an organized Jewish community in America. . . . [T]he Hebrew language is not only a means of imparting knowledge, but at the very soul of Jewish culture."[295] Also in 1941, the Brandeis Camp Institute opened in Amherst, New Hampshire. This leadership training program, which was soon relocated to the Los Angeles area by founding director Shlomo Bardin, served college-age young adults, combining experiential learning, recreation, the arts, and distinctive Shabbat celebration that nurtured Jewish identity.[296] In 1944, the Boston Hebrew Teachers College launched Camp Yavneh to "enrich and deepen the knowledge of students of the Hebrew Teachers College and to foster the use of Hebrew outside the classroom."[297]

The Conservative movement entered the field of Jewish educational camping, opening Camp Ramah in Wisconsin in 1947. The Ramah initiative followed the establishment, in 1945, of LTF (Leaders Training Fellowship)—part of a ten-year plan adopted by JTS—which aimed "to identify and cultivate the best young people within Conservative synagogues and lead them into Jewish public service."[298] Camping, which represented an opportunity for an intensive experience in Jewish living, was an extension of this goal. Chicago-area rabbinic and lay leadership made it possible to acquire a camp in Wisconsin, which opened as Ramah (literally, "high place") in 1947. The Ramah program, committed to Jewish living, Hebrew, and study, used the summer months to "shore up" the inadequate amount of time otherwise available for Jewish education.

Ramah was most heavily influenced by Cejwin, Massad, and Achvah, camps attended by those who conceived and implemented its program.[299] Among Ramah's distinguishing features, from its inception and beyond, were: (1) educational supervision by the Jewish Theological Seminary's Teachers Institute; (2) formal study for campers as well as staff; and (3) a professor-in-residence, typically from JTS. Burton Cohen, a future Ramah director and professor of education at JTS, and Yochanan Muffs, a future Seminary professor of Bible, were among the initial cohort of campers at Ramah-Wisconsin in 1947.[300] Additional Ramah camps were established in the Poconos (1950), New England (1953), California (1956), Canada (1960), and the Berkshires (1961) within the next fourteen years.[301]

Starting in 1947, NFTY launched a number of short conclaves and leadership institutes at several camps. In 1951, the UAHC Chicago Federation approved the idea of acquiring a property for camp use and, soon thereafter, a private Jewish camp in Oconomowoc, Wisconsin, was purchased. The UAHC camp, known as the Union Institute (later Olin-Sang-Ruby Union Institute), held institutes of two weeks or less. Union Institutes initially focused on teen and adult populations; an experimental one-week session for eleven- and twelve-year-olds was introduced in 1954.[302] Hebrew played no role at the UAHC camp, nor—in the early years—did Zionism. The worship experience and spirituality were emphasized. As was the case with Ramah, Union Institute became a camping movement, with Camp Saratoga (later Swig) opening in California, followed by three more camps by 1958. Union camps, unlike Ramah, functioned with local autonomy.[303] The opening of Ramah and of the Union Institute introduced denominationalism to Jewish camping. Of the new Jewish camps established between 1940 and 1960, nearly 40 percent featured educational and religious aims, compared with 5 percent prior to 1940.[304]

The proliferation of Jewish residential camps coast to coast in the 1940s and 1950s provided frameworks for experiencing Jewish living around the clock, even if for only weeks or months at a time. In addition to the campers, many staff members of these camps were deeply influenced by their summer experiences. Many alumni of these camps became advocates—as rabbis and educators, as well as volunteers on boards of synagogues and Jewish communal agencies—of more intensive and expansive Jewish educational experiences for children and youth, and they sought broader opportunities for adult Jewish living and learning.[305] The informal mode of camp prayer services, both at Ramah and the Union Institute, was to influence public worship in the synagogues of the Conservative and Reform movements in years to come.

Jewish youth groups continued to grow after World War II, not only as Jewish educational settings but as social networks. Already at the first NFTY convention in 1939, it had been emphasized that "it is better for young people to meet one another under wholesome auspices than to listen to a dozen sermons against intermarriage."[306] New entries to the field included the Conservative United Synagogue Youth (USY), initiated in 1951, and the Orthodox National Conference of Synagogue Youth, created in 1959.[307] Jewish educators frequently encouraged students to participate in mutually reinforcing school, youth group, and residential summer camp experiences.

During the settlement house era, in the early decades of the twentieth century, a variety of Jewish community centers was established, often dedicated to the Americanization of Jewish immigrants.[308] In a letter of resignation from the board of the Educational Alliance, one of the largest settlement houses on New York's Lower East Side, Solomon Schechter had presciently noted that "the great question before the Jewish community is not so much the Americanizing of the Russian Jew as his Judaizing. We have now quite sufficient agencies for his Americanization. But the problem is whether we are able to keep the immigrant within Judaism after he has become Americanized. . . . There cannot be the least doubt that what the immigrant loses quickest in this country is his Judaism."[309] Schechter's comments early in the twentieth century—which had animated the educational work in which he engaged—were to be loudly echoed in connection with the agenda and activities of Jewish Community Centers by mid-century.

During the Great Depression, Jewish Community Center services to the entire community became common. Many professionals at JCCs saw themselves as agents in social reconstruction.[310] As men were called to military service in World War II and large numbers of women entered the labor force, many Jewish Community Centers organized nursery schools and kindergartens to provide care for the children of working mothers. Early childhood programs became an integral part of the centers' postwar activities.

With the move to the suburbs, new Jewish Community Centers were built in areas of Jewish population. In the two decades after World War II, $125 million was invested in new JCC facilities.[311] With the era of immigration at a close and synagogues becoming principal centers of contact and connection among Jews, the Jewish Welfare Board, the umbrella organization of the Jewish Community Centers, commissioned a study, conducted from 1945 to 1947, to articulate the mission of Jewish Community Centers at mid-century.[312] The study, known as the Janowsky Report, was released in 1948. Oscar Janowsky, its author, noted: "The Survey revealed that nearly 20 percent of the agencies did not report a single project or activity of specific Jewish content. More than 23 percent reported no Jewish programs for children; close to 35 percent reported none for adults; and at least 55 percent indicated none for youth. Few indeed were the Centers in which an atmosphere of intensive Jewish interest or activity prevailed."[313] While calling upon centers to advance what Schechter had termed the "Judaizing cause," the report did not offer guidance as to how the centers might achieve the recommended outcome.

Jewish Education for College Students and Adults

By the 1930s, Harry Wolfson and Salo Baron had become eminent scholars in Jewish studies at Harvard and Columbia, respectively, but it was the ethnic studies current of the late 1960s that generated a proliferation of Jewish studies courses at hundreds of American universities. Sociologist Egon Mayer observed that the 1960s stand out as a time when minority groups in America achieved a heightened awareness and assertiveness in a tolerant host society.[314] Reflecting the growing interest in ethnic studies that began with the black pride movement and rapidly extended to other groups, the number of full-time university positions in Jewish studies rose from twelve in 1945 to sixty-five by 1965.[315] In addition to the growth in university-level Judaic studies courses emerging from the ethnic pride current, the excitement generated by the remarkable events of the June 1967 Six-Day War brought a dramatic escalation in the number of and participation levels in programs for American high school and college students in Israel.

For adult Jewish education, the 1940s marked the beginning of a period of growth. The Conservative movement's National Academy for Adult Jewish Studies was established in 1940, followed in 1948 by the founding of the Department of Continuing Education of the UAHC. B'nai B'rith initiated adult "Institutes of Judaism" in 1948.[316] With such programs proliferating in the 1950s and early 1960s, the American Association for Jewish Education in 1965 convened the first national conference on Jewish adult education in the United States. Analyzing a survey of professionals—rabbis, Bureau of Jewish Education directors, Federation executives, and leaders of nine national organizations—who were questioned about the emerging field of adult Jewish education, Oscar Janowsky commented that, though there was ample evidence that programs of adult Jewish learning were on the rise, the "aims and purposes [of adult education programs] are unclear, if not nebulous."[317] The escalation of programs was consistent with the expansion of adult education during the 1950s and 1960s, generally as a result of more leisure time and a higher level of education.

The Havurah Movement

Havurot, or fellowship groups, were a Jewish expression of 1960s and 1970s youth culture. Young activist Jews who had grown up in suburbia created alternative Jewish frameworks for prayer, study, and friendship. *Havurot* emphasized the equality of all who belonged. *Havurah* members, often from large Conservative or Reform synagogues, saw the large congregations with which they were familiar as vapid and lacking in spiritual substance. Committed to such causes as the peace movement, civil rights, and feminism, those attracted to *havurot* also identified proudly as Jews. The *havurah* was countercultural vis-à-vis the Judaism of participants' parents and American youth culture.

Havurot were established in the late 1960s and early 1970s in Somerville (outside Boston), New York, Washington, D.C., and Philadelphia.[318] In *havurah* groups, which were not affiliated with any denomination, participants resolved issues of ritual practice by consensus. The *havurah* movements' experimentation with Jewish ritual is captured in *The Jewish Catalog* (first volume, 1973; second, 1976; third, 1980).

By the end of the 1970s, synagogues had recognized the value of small fellowships, and many congregations created synagogue-based *havurot* for purposes of study, social action, holiday celebrations, and other needs. Camp alumni accustomed to less formality in worship, coupled with the *havurah* movement, gradually influenced the style of prayer services in large congregations. As *havurah* members of the late 1960s and early 1970s aged, some of the *havurot* they had established were transformed into *minyanim* (prayer assemblies; alternative congregations).[319]

Admission of Women to Rabbinical Training

Mordecai Kaplan, long a champion of the equal participation of women in synagogue life, initiated the public ceremony of bat mitzvah—on the occasion of his daughter Judith's bat mitzvah—in 1922. In 1951, the Society for the Advancement of Judaism, which Kaplan had helped found and where he served as rabbi for decades, began the practice of regularly calling women to the Torah and counting them as part of the minyan of ten adult worshipers. Though by no means ubiquitous in the Conservative movement, bat mitzvah ceremonies became far more widespread in the suburban congregations of the 1950s and 1960s than they had been pre–World War II.

In the late 1960s and early 1970s, the feminist movement and the *havurot* led to the formation of women's prayer and study groups. In this climate, the Reform movement began to admit women to the HUC rabbinical training program in the late 1960s; in 1972, Sally Priesand, an HUC graduate, became the first woman ordained as a rabbi in the United States. The Reconstructionist Rabbinical College, launched in 1968 under the leadership of Ira Eisenstein, son-in-law and close disciple of Mordecai Kaplan, admitted women to rabbinical training from its inception. Serious agitation for the ordination of women in the Conservative movement began in 1972; a majority opinion of the Rabbinical Assembly Law Committee ruled, in 1973, that women could be counted as part of a minyan. After much rancorous debate, women were formally admitted to rabbinical study at JTS, in 1982, with the first graduate earning ordination in 1985.[320]

Survival Concerns

Despite the many positive trends in Jewish life and Jewish education in the 1950s and 1960s, ominous challenges to continuing Jewish vitality were present. In 1957, the United States Census Bureau, regarding family birthrates among Catholics, Protestants, and Jews, reported: Catholics, 3.1 children; Protestants, 2.8; Jews, 2.1.[321] Indeed, with the end of the post–World War II baby boom, Jewish school enrollment declined by the mid-1970s to under 400,000—from a peak of nearly 590,000 in 1962. A 1964 *Look* magazine article on the "vanishing American Jew" pointed to a decreasing birthrate and increasing rates of intermarriage as evidence of the erosion of Jewish life in the United States. Evidence of escalating intermarriage was confirmed by the National Jewish Population Survey of 1971, which reported that the rate of such marriages had risen from under 7 percent in the 1950s to 31 percent for marriages between 1966 and 1970.[322]

In his widely discussed 1973 book *The Ambivalent American Jew,* sociologist Charles Liebman expressed the fundamental tension in Jewish life in the United States: "The American Jew is torn between two sets of values—those of integration and acceptance into American society and those of Jewish group survival. The values appear to me to be incompatible."[323]

The vision of integration articulated by Benderly, Kaplan, and generations of Jewish educators was, it seemed, more elusive than once imagined. In addition to a declining birthrate in a growing American population—and intermarriage—geographic mobility and diffusion portended diminished Jewish political strength. Moreover, the indifference of many ostensible "allies" to the plight of Israel in 1967 and vulnerability engendered by the 1973 Yom Kippur War contributed to a mounting communal insecurity.

As Jewish communal leaders spoke the language of "Jewish survival," the focus of congregational education became Jewish identity—"to make young people feel more Jewish."[324] Because Jewish identity building is common to many settings, a grassroots initiative, Coalition for Alternatives in Jewish Education (CAJE), was organized in 1975 as a forum for networking in Jewish education. Its national conference has been held each summer since 1976.

Yet it appeared that these strategies were ill suited to achieving survival. Studies published in 1975 and 1976 claimed that a minimum threshold of instructional hours of Jewish schooling—3,000 according to one study and 1,000 according to another—was required to impart adult religious identification.[325] One researcher concluded: "The type of Jewish education received by over 80 percent of those American Jews who have received any Jewish education has been a waste of time."[326]

One response to mounting survival concern was increased funding of Jewish education, particularly day school education. In 1974, Charles Zibbell, associate director of the Council of Jewish Federations and Welfare Funds, noted a marked shift in Federation attitude and practice toward day schools: "[I]t was but a short time ago that dozens of Federations were actually on record as philosophically opposed to Day Schools. The situation has changed radically. There is no Federation that is philosophically opposed to Day Schools today. . . . We are at a point now where 30 percent of all of the funds allocated for Jewish education by Federations go to Jewish Day Schools."[327]

Beyond the matter of hours of instruction, Walter Ackerman raised a more basic question in 1975: What—besides mere survival—was the goal of American Jewish education? He stated:

> Education, in its most fundamental sense, . . . is the expression of a sensibility to a standard and represents the attempt of a society to mold the character of its members in accordance with an ideal. That ideal is not only a statement of what man ought

to be, it is also the criterion which determines the materials and methods used to make him that way. I would suggest that Jewish education, except in Orthodox quarters, . . . has not been informed by such an ideal. One can argue with some cogency, I believe, that until such an ideal is articulated, efforts at the "improvement" of Jewish education will remain little more than patchwork mechanics which only fall short of any serious mark. . . .

[T]he idea of survival is not a sufficiently fundamental or basic idea on which to build a program of education.[328]

The development of a vision of Jewish education grounded in purposeful Jewish existence—the "ideal" that Ackerman recognized as lacking—remained troublingly elusive, notwithstanding a generation of growth and expansion.

What were the goals and purposes of Jewish survivalism? Why be different? Why be Jewish? These were among the central questions in defining the work of Jewish education, viewed as a primary agent of "Jewish continuity" late in the twentieth century.

CHAPTER SIX

Educational Trends at the Close
of the Twentieth Century, 1975–2000

In the last quarter of the twentieth century, Jewish education emerged as a focus of Jewish communal and philanthropic efforts to address the challenge to "Jewish continuity" in the United States. This chapter reflects the explicit connection between various educational initiatives and Jewish continuity concerns of the generation. Many Jewish Federations established Jewish Continuity Commissions, and philanthropic foundations and individual funders with interest in Jewish life came to play a more significant role in financing and shaping Jewish educational projects. Evidence of intensified Jewish learning and living was readily available, as was evidence of declining Jewish population and diminishing levels of Jewish engagement among many Jews.

Jewish day school enrollment continued to increase, reaching 185,000 students from the four-year-old preschool level through high school.[329] Participation in Israel experience programs by students was defined as a "birthright" and made available at no charge to those who had not previously experienced Israel as part of an organized peer program. Efforts were made to expand residential camping as a Jewish educational option; initiatives to recruit and train recent college graduates for service as Jewish educators were launched; programs of systematic, comprehensive adult learning attracted growing numbers of participants; and congregational strategies to nurture communities of Jewish learning were piloted.

In a superb article on late-twentieth-century trends in Jewish education, Jack Wertheimer elaborates upon a number of significant currents, including: the growth of early childhood education programs; the boom in Jewish studies programs on college campuses and the revitalization of Hillel; a more holistic approach to Jewish education, embracing formal and informal educational experiences; family education in a variety of settings—including Jewish Community Centers, schools, and retreat centers; the proliferation of adult study opportunities; the impact—albeit affecting a modest percentage of the population pool—of Jewish residential camping; expanded Israel trips, including Birthright Israel (a partnership between North American Jewish philanthropists, Jewish Federations, and the Israeli government for American Jewish college students to experience Israel on organized ten-day trips at no charge); and foundation initiatives in funding broad issues in a systemic fashion.[330]

Many trends in Wertheimer's list were responses to findings in the 1990 National Jewish Population Survey, which indicated that the intermarriage rate had reached 52 percent over the most recent five-year period (a figure challenged by some as overstating a rate that stood "only" at 43 percent).[331] The data revealed an association between more intensive Jewish education (day school vs. several times a week vs. once a week) and less intermarriage. Such an association could not consider factors such as patterns of Jewish family behavior. Moreover, the data underscored that even among those with the most Jewish education, there remained, albeit at significantly lower levels, a considerable incidence of intermarriage.

Even before the release of the National Jewish Population Survey, the Commission on Jewish Education in North America, convened by philanthropist Morton Mandel, issued a report, *A Time to Act*, which suggested Jewish education as an antidote to the contemporary malaise of American Jewry, which expressed itself in growing numbers of Jews no longer finding Judaism meaningful to their lives.[332] Books such as *Why Be Different?*[333] and *Why Be Jewish?*[334] suggested compelling answers to these questions. The Mandel Foundation undertook a "visions" of Jewish education project, to articulate multiple ideals from which educators might create coherent curricula.

Trends in School-Based Education

Though a fairly constant 35–40 percent of school-aged children were enrolled in some type of Jewish education in any given year throughout this period,[335] there were shifts in the type of schools that they attended. Among Orthodox Jews, day school education had by the 1980s become almost universal, and birthrates were high. The trend of increasing numbers of students in day schools continued, and within the day school universe, "community" nondenominational day schools were a growing phenomenon. Continuing disaffection with the quality of public education, combined with economic prosperity, made private schooling an option of choice for many non-Orthodox Jews. In addition to the core group seeking day school education because of religious commitment were families for whom the Jewish day school was a place of educational excellence combined with commitment to positive values, character development, and wholesome community for students as well as parents. In a climate that some described as "post-denominational," allegiance to Conservative or Reform ideology gave way to the development of a broad enough population base to ensure the goal of educational excellence.

Besides the Torah Umesorah, Solomon Schechter, and Progressive Alliance of Reform Day Schools networks, networks of pluralistic day schools, representing approximately 10 percent of schools and of student enrollment, emerged. Community elementary schools were organized as RAVSAK (an acronym for the Hebrew name of the Jewish Community Day School Network). In 1999, the North American Association of Jewish High Schools, NAAJHS, was formed. Consisting chiefly of community day high schools, this network had more than twenty member schools within three years of its establishment. Its programs included joint student activities, in addition to collaboration among educational professionals.

A 2000 study of day schools by the Avi Chai Foundation showed that 80 percent of the 185,000 students, pre-K through twelfth grade, enrolled in the country's 670 day schools were in Orthodox schools and that more than half of the total number of day school enrollees were in the state of New York. That the day school phenomenon, however, was not exclusively the concern of Orthodox institutional leadership was reflected in the emergence of the Partnership for Excellence in Jewish Education (PEJE). This consortium of mostly other-than-Orthodox philanthropists promotes access to and the quality of day school education.

The end of the twentieth century saw the establishment of a number of day high schools, particularly community, nondenominational high schools, including a boarding school in Greensboro, North Carolina. While such high schools primarily served non-Orthodox populations, some Orthodox families, disenchanted with the "move to the right" in Orthodox yeshiva high schools and attracted by the readiness of some community schools to accommodate a "yeshiva track," enrolled their children in these schools. Elementary day schools in the non-Orthodox sector had become well established, and teen population was at a peak, as a result of the post–World War II baby boom. These conditions, combined with the growing trend toward private education, fostered an openness to the idea of Jewish day high school education and contributed to the proliferation of day high schools.

At the close of the twentieth century, government financial support for the education of students attending day schools, whether through voucher programs or through funding of assorted educational services, continued to be vigorously debated within the Jewish community.[336] In a climate of public discussion and government action in the domains of special-education services and accommodations for students with developmental issues, special-needs initiatives were launched in schools, camps, and youth-group settings. Such programs were often spearheaded by parents seeking inclusion for their children. As in the public sector, the high cost of providing special-education services sometimes created tensions between the desire of parents of special-needs learners for a full range of accommodation mechanisms in venues of their choice, and the readiness of schools to provide the required range of services.[337] Beyond the intrinsic desirability of embracing all who seek Jewish educational opportunity, it remained to be seen whether the tapering off of the echo of the baby boom—and a decline in the number of "available" Jewish children of school age—might encourage institutions to invest more substantially in serving a broader range of participants.

Reflecting on the growth of non-Orthodox day schools, which, by the late twentieth century, held a 20 percent "market share" of day school enrollment, Barry Chazan suggested that these schools were transformed versions of the intensive supplementary schools of an earlier era.[338] Earlier, the agenda of congregational schools had consisted of nurturing synagogue skills, teaching the coexistence of Jewishness and Americanism, and encouraging an intensively Jewish lifestyle. Those concerned with the third objective had, by the last decades of the twentieth century, moved on to day schools. Students in day schools studied Hebrew language—typically, five days a week—and classical Jewish texts, primarily Bible, at levels no longer offered in supplementary schools. In addition to discrete subjects of Jewish study, many liberal Jewish day schools consciously undertook to develop "integrated" curricula, synthesizing subjects of Jewish and general education.[339] In response to member families' expressed needs, many part-time schools sponsored by Conservative congregations modified their traditional three-day six-hour-a-week standard in favor of two weekly sessions. Many Reform congregations had implemented two weekly sessions. By the close of the century, there was little structural difference between the congregational schools operated by the two major denominations sponsoring such schools.

So ubiquitous had day school education become among Orthodox Jews, that virtually no Orthodox afternoon schools remained, save Chabad-sponsored outreach programs. With the growth of day schools and the transformation of afternoon schools to two-day-a-week programs, the profession once imagined for full-time Talmud Torah teachers was available only in day schools. Afternoon schools assembled eclectic faculties, including public school teachers, college students, congregants, day school teachers, and synagogue clergy.

A major study conducted by the Board of Jewish Education of Greater New York in the mid-1980s questioned the efficacy of congregational schooling as it was then constituted. The study's report, "Jewish Supplementary Schooling: An Educational System in Need of Change,"[340] urged that family education and informal education be made integral to supplementary education and that training and educational career opportunities be developed to attract and retain qualified personnel for the type of education recommended.

Family education, which looks to the family as the unit receiving education, became a focus of Jewish educational thought in the 1980s and 1990s.[341] The Whizin Institute at the University of Judaism conducted an annual weeklong seminar for educators, disseminating best practices in this emerging field. In Boston, the combined Jewish Philanthropies (Federation) subsidized family educators in congregations throughout the community. Supplementary schools were not the only educational institutions seeking greater parental involvement in Jewish study and other Jewish living experiences. Programs of early childhood Jewish education afforded opportunities for Jewish educational engagement with young children, parents, and families. "Nursery schools," accordingly, came to be redefined as "early childhood education centers."

Congregational Change
and Adult Education Initiatives

At the end of the twentieth century, many congregational change initiatives were launched, often including reimagining Jewish education. In the 1990s, Joseph Reimer of Brandeis University chronicled a model of effective school-based Jewish education in a congregation that had apparently transformed itself into a community of learning.[342] Isa Aron of the Rhea Hirsch School of Education at HUC-JIR, Los Angeles, led a systematic project, "The Experiment in Congregational Education," to reconceptualize congregational education. In Aron's vision, synagogues needed to reengineer themselves into congregations of learners: "A congregation of learners is a center for authentic Jewish learning—learning that is viewed as a lifelong endeavor that grows out of the life of the community, and which, in turn, strengthens the community. The congregation of learners is both a means to an end and an end in itself; it is an instrument for enculturating individual members for participation in Jewish life. But it is also a model for Jewish communities."[343] The congregation as an organic community would, it was projected, provide a context and a stimulus for lifelong Jewish learning. On another track, such adult education frameworks as the Florence Melton Adult Mini School (1986), Boston's Meah—literally, "one hundred," referring to one hundred hours of study—program (1994), and the Wexner Foundation Heritage program (1985), serving thousands of participants over a two-year period of well-defined, substantial study, sought to effectuate sociocultural transformation of the American Jewish community through adult Jewish learning. Yet another framework of adult learning was the synagogue-based adult bat mitzvah course, often extending over one or two years. Scores of Elderhostel programs offered people over fifty-five the opportunity to spend a week in residence at a college pursuing topics of Jewish interest. With high levels of education and economic well-being, education as a leisure pursuit was attractive to segments of adult Jewry. Some parents who sent their children to a day school but who lacked Jewish education themselves enrolled in adult study to better relate to their children's experience.

Hebrew teachers' colleges, which had been created earlier in the century to train teachers for Talmud Torah schools, reinvented themselves to meet new needs. Hebrew College in Boston, for example—which dropped "Teachers" from its name—served as a community, adult education resource, a strategy common among these colleges. As the field of Jewish communal service developed—with thousands of Jewish "civil service" personnel employed by Jewish Federations and affiliated agencies—the colleges initiated schools or departments of Jewish communal service. Though teacher training programs all but disappeared, graduate training programs in Jewish educational administration were established at all the Hebrew teachers' colleges.

Articulating New Visions of Jewish Education

Earlier in the century, the congruence of American and Jewish values was emphasized; at the end of the twentieth century, visions of Jewish education focused more on Jewish particularity. Michael Meyer, a Jewish historian and professor at HUC-Cincinnati observed: "Once it seemed important to show how Jews were similar to Christians and how Jewish traditions anticipated American values enshrined in the Constitution. Judaism was taught via the catechism as a species subordinated to the genus 'religion,' which also included Christianity. That integrationist perspective did not harm Jewish continuity as long as Jews lived in social separation. Today it is clear that an educated Jew must know Judaism and Jewish values not only in their relationship to Christianity and American culture, but also as distinguishable from them."[344]

Meyer opined that anchorage in Judaism enables the Jewishly educated Jew to reach outward to the broader community "across a boundary that Jewish education has clearly marked."[345] For Meyer, it is grounding in distinctiveness that allows for engagement without loss of Jewish selfhood with the universal human community. Jewish educators in the past wanted to establish that Jewish values were "at one" with the prevailing American ethos; but the task of contemporary Jewish education, suggested Meyer, is to be able to distinguish Judaism's uniqueness.

Meyer's approach was reflected not only in such ideological pronouncements as the Reform movement's Pittsburgh Platform of 1999, which re-embraced many aspects of Jewish tradition rejected in the Pittsburgh Platform of 1885, but in curricula developed for children. In a work on changing emphases in texts written by Jewish authors for teaching Bible to Jewish children over the course of the twentieth century, Penny Schine Gold observes that, while earlier generations' textbooks relied heavily on Christian models and pointed to the shared, "universal" text of the Bible, late-twentieth-century works drew explicitly upon rabbinic literature. Parallel to curricula presenting a uniquely Jewish approach to understanding the Bible was a proliferation of publications of collected rabbinic stories.[346]

Another vision of contemporary Jewish education was articulated by Moshe Greenberg, a Bible scholar and son of former JTS vice chancellor Simon Greenberg: "A Jewish education worthy of the name will address the hunger of the learner to know 'whence he came and whither he is going.' It will furnish him with value-concepts by which to infuse raw experience with meaning and order. The success of a Jewish education is measured by its adequacy in accompanying the learner through life as a treasury of concepts lending meaning to private and public experience."[347]

School-based Jewish education, particularly in sectors other than the Orthodox, embraced ideas like those of Meyer and Greenberg, comparing Jewish texts and the core values embedded in them with the traditions of other groups and reflecting on Jewish teachings as sources of personal meaning. Students were offered a "tool kit" of Jewish teachings as sources of group identity and personal meaning, an approach most dramatically reflected in community day high schools—from Boston, to Washington, D.C., to Los Angeles—which often, quite intentionally, hired faculty with diverse Jewish religious ideologies to make accessible the range of meaning found by serious Jews in Jewish teaching. Rather than one ideal, multiple paths of Jewish engagement were displayed, discussed, and validated by their inclusion. The long-term effect of this approach remains to be seen.

While Orthodox institutions maintained their traditional emphasis on classical texts and observance of divinely ordained *mitzvot,* American-born yeshiva educators, well aware of the prevailing cultural milieu, gave more attention to *hashkafah,* worldview, distinguishing a traditional Jewish perspective from societal norms. In the Orthodox sector, as a growing disparity between "traditional" Torah Umesorah schools and more "integrated"—i.e., more inclined to synthesis—yeshiva schools developed, the Association of Modern Orthodox Day Schools (AMODS) was established.[348] Affiliated with Yeshiva University, the AMODS network included eighty schools at the close of the twentieth century.

In a work published in 2000, Steven M. Cohen and Arnold Eisen observed that the first language of most American Jews is individualism.

Accordingly, they advised, those who assume educational leadership must function as "operators of a transit system. A bus must be ready and waiting at the bus stop at the exact moment that the prospective Jewish rider appears. The fleet must be sufficiently large to be there whenever wanted, and it must be sufficiently diverse to take account of the diverse tastes and needs of its potential clientele."[349] Among the vehicles deployed at the end of the twentieth century were computer and Internet technology. Religious movements, colleges of Jewish studies—transformed Hebrew teachers' colleges of earlier in the century, operating independently but networked as the Association of Institutions of Higher Learning for Jewish Education—and a host of other educational providers made Jewish learning accessible online for students of all ages. Recognition of what Cohen and Eisen termed the "sovereign Jewish self" informed the efforts of those who envisioned making Jewish educational opportunity more readily available.

Partnership 2000 and (Re)Emphasis of Hebrew

The 1990s saw the emergence of "Partnership 2000," a series of twinning linkages between Israeli municipalities and various American Jewish Federations. Within those partnerships, educational initiatives between Israeli schools and American Jewish schools were launched. These joint ventures typically brought faculty, and sometimes students, together, often around questions of the nature and meaning of Jewish peoplehood and core Jewish values. A century after Ahad Ha'am suggested that a critical mass of Jews constituting a majority population in the Land of Israel might resolve the malaise of Judaism in the modern world, the legatees of his thinking—in Israel and in the United States—were working jointly to meet the continuing challenge of articulating the meaning of Jewish identity in post-traditional society. On both sides of these partnerships, Jewish communities aggregating 75 percent of world Jewry sensed the need for such definition, knowing that a guiding purpose is essential to coherent, effective action.

Renewed declarations of the importance of Hebrew language literacy were sounded in the 1990s. For example, the Statement of Principles for Reform Judaism, adopted at the 1999 Pittsburgh Convention of the Central Conference of American Rabbis, affirmed "the importance of studying Hebrew, the language of Torah and Jewish liturgy, that we may draw closer to our people's sacred texts."[350] Though Isaac Mayer Wise had given expression to the same principle 130 years earlier, the instructional programs of UAHC schools had not, over the twentieth century, nurtured substantial Hebrew literacy. It remains to be seen what impact this summons of the new Pittsburgh Platform might have on curriculum and instruction in the educational settings of Reform Jewry.

In the mid-1990s, Ismar Schorsch, then chancellor of the Jewish Theological Seminary, in a pamphlet describing the seven core values of Conservative Judaism, identified "Hebrew as the irreplaceable language of Jewish expression" as one such core value.[351] He urged that Hebrew must "emerge as the common and unifying language of the Jewish people."[352] At a time when Conservative congregational education—the prevalent educational setting in the Conservative movement—was, for increasing numbers of students, being restructured from three weekly sessions to two weekly contacts, it was unclear whether—outside the day school—this agenda could be actualized.

Ironically, declarations about the importance of Hebrew came at a time of access to an ever-expanding array of Jewish classical works in English translation. The Talmud, classical commentaries, responsa, codes, and aggadic texts are all available in English. This reality, combined with decreased instructional time for Hebrew studies, suggests that the pronouncements of elites about the importance of Hebrew were unlikely to be "translated" into facts on the ground.

Escalating Participation Levels in University Jewish Studies and Post–High School Yeshiva Education Programs

By 1998, Jewish civilization was being taught or researched at more than 700 American institutions of higher learning.[353] Although the 2000–2001 National Jewish Population Survey indicated that 41 percent of Jewish undergraduates took at least one course in Jewish studies during their college years, it is important to bear in mind that the academic analysis of aspects of Jewish civilization is neither designed nor presented with the aim of nurturing Jewish identity. As a noted academic reminds us: "The university is not devoted to promoting the ideals of Jewish civilization; it is . . . devoted to a dispassionate analysis of culture per se. . . . Jewish academics—the major contact most of our young people will have with Jewish thought and history on a sophisticated level—owe neither institutional nor intellectual loyalty to any part of the Jewish community."[354] At the close of the twentieth century, a revitalized Hillel Foundation (independent of its parent organization, B'nai B'rith) sought to meet—and, for many, to create—Jewish educational needs of an estimated 400,000 Jewish college students. At such campuses as Harvard, the University of Pennsylvania, Brown, and UCLA, capital projects aggregating tens of millions of dollars were undertaken by Hillel Foundations to create more attractive Hillel facilities to provide expanded student services and promote Jewish engagement.

By 2000, an estimated 18,000 post–high school young men—in addition to the more than 150,000 boys and girls in Orthodox Jewish day schools—were enrolled in yeshivot and *kolellim*.[355] Of this number, approximately 2,350 studied at the Beth Medrash Govoha in Lakewood, and 1,500 were at the United Talmudical Seminary of the Satmar Hasidim.[356] The establishment of small, activist *kolellim* emerged in cities including Boca Raton, Atlanta, Pittsburgh, Chicago, and Los Angeles, in which full-time, devoutly Orthodox Talmudists devoted significant time to community education, engaging in study with Orthodox coreligionists as well as non-traditionalist segments of Jewry. By the 1990s, with the maturation of a generation schooled in yeshivot and, in many cases, engaged in continuing Jewish learning, the study of *daf yomi,* a daily page of Talmud text on a cycle that covers the entire Babylonian Talmud over seven and a half years, had become common in Orthodox settings throughout the United States. In September 1997, 20,000 men gathered in New York's Madison Square Garden to celebrate the completion of such a cycle. In addition to a growing number of *kolel* participants and ordinary professionals engaged in Talmud study on a daily basis, thousands of Orthodox American Jewish young men and women studied each year in yeshivot and seminaries in Israel. A year or two of study in Israel upon high school graduation was encouraged by yeshiva high schools as a rite of passage.

The Sovereign Self

Structures of Jewish corporate society—organized communities with coercive power, characteristic of medieval and early modern Jewish life elsewhere—never held sway in America. Through the first half of the twentieth century, however, immigrant ties, the specter of anti-Semitism, and then the Holocaust and support of the emerging State of Israel sustained strong communal bonds. By the end of the twentieth century, such links were wearing thin. A 1998 survey found that just 52 percent of respondents agreed with the statement: "I look at the entire Jewish community as my extended Jewish family," and only 47 percent agreed that "I have a special responsibility to take care of Jews in need around the world."[357]

The sovereign self, an expression of American individualism, was already evidenced in the inability of the early *kehillot kodesh*—synagogue-communities—to maintain communal discipline early in the American Jewish experience. Nonetheless, Jews felt an ethnic kinship, manifest in helping successive waves of immigrants and banding together to assist Jews in other parts of the world. Nurturing this collective responsibility was an issue for educational consideration at the close of the twentieth century. Not only is Judaism as community-centered versus Judaism as individual spiritual journey at issue; the very question, "Who is a Jew?" is at issue. If there is to be a communal focus, the community and its boundaries are a matter that each educational system must define. The decision of the Reform movement in 1983 to adopt the principle of patrilineal descent,[358] for example, challenges groups that do not endorse this approach to determine how they will educate with regard to recognizing (or not) those who may be Jewish by this definition. Indeed, for those schools that only admit "Jews," the issue is all the more stark. For schools of all streams, intermarriage raises a host of educational issues—from holiday season celebrations with family members of other faiths to the participation of non-Jewish parents in Jewish rituals.

Education and Ideology

The texts from the broad universe of Jewish teaching selected for study; the decision to teach or not to teach Hebrew—and, if teaching Hebrew, the goals of such instruction; an emphasis on peoplehood or on matters of individual spirituality: all are rooted in ideological approaches to the core values of Jewish life. Israel education, for example, may mean to some an emphasis on biblical Israel; to others, the yearning for Zion through the ages; to others, the emergence of modern Zionism; and to others, contemporary Israeli life and society. Ideology will further determine focal themes: religion, politics, geography, universalism vs. particularism, messianism, and Israel and the diaspora; and ideology will guide the choice of texts and the meaning ascribed to those texts. The Bible may be studied as God's promise of the Land of Israel to the Jewish people, or as testimony to the importance of the Land of Israel in Jewish civilization over the millennia. Given the vast body of Jewish learning and limited instructional time in any educational setting, the very question of whether or to what extent to include Israel education in a course of study is itself a matter of ideological outlook.

In the last quarter of the twentieth century, thousands of Holocaust survivors, after years of silence, shared their stories. Prominent examples include the film *Schindler's List*; the United States Holocaust Memorial Museum in Washington, D.C., along with dozens of local museums and Holocaust memorials; and the work of the Shoah Foundation in gathering and making available the testimonies of tens of thousands of survivors. The Israeli-initiated International March of the Living program enrolls thousands of Jewish teens from many countries each year to march from Auschwitz to Birkenau on Yom HaShoah (Holocaust Remembrance Day), and thereafter travel to Israel for Yom Ha'atzmaut (Israel's Day of Independence). This program reflects the ideological underpinnings of Jewish educational choices. For some, the experience might be approached as the ultimate Zionist call: there is no future for diaspora Jewry; Israel is the only answer to the ever-present threat to Jewish survival. Others might emphasize the peoplehood of world Jewry, focusing on shared historical experiences and engaging in real-time, international Jewish youth encounters. Others might focus on the dramatic effects of "righteous Gentiles" and take a universalist social action approach, turning to efforts on behalf of oppressed people. Passivity and resistance, power and powerlessness, religion or denial of religion—these and other issues are embedded in any Holocaust curriculum and are magnified in the intensive March of the Living program.

In order to help day schools, religious schools, and early childhood centers reflect upon and articulate their mission and goals, the Los Angeles Bureau of Jewish Education initiated a pioneering school accreditation process in the 1990s. To remain eligible for communal funding, schools were expected to periodically engage in a comprehensive self-study process, articulating their mission and relating their curricula and instructional choices to the goals identified.[359] Visiting teams of educators spent several days on campus, relating their observations to the self-study compendium developed by each institution and offering recommendations to better align curriculum and instruction with each school's stated vision. From 1994 to 2000, seventy schools in the Los Angeles area undertook the accreditation process, and additional communities were exploring introduction of similar protocols.

Trends and Challenges

Though there have been cyclical trends in Hebrew language education, ranging from decoding for purposes of prayer-book reading to language immersion, and ebbs and flows in adult learning initiatives, certain aspects of Jewish education in the United States have consistently moved in particular directions. As reflected throughout these pages, one such movement has been the expansion of responsibility for the provision and advancement of Jewish education for school-age children. Colonial- and early-national-period notions of parental responsibility gave way to benevolent societies, synagogues, and federated communities sponsoring Jewish educational opportunities. By the end of the twentieth century, major philanthropic foundations and community endowments were devoting tens of millions of dollars to making a variety of Jewish educational experiences more broadly accessible.

Another area of forward movement has been women's education. In Eastern Europe, school-based Jewish education for girls was a phenomenon of the early twentieth century; Jewish education in the United States not only included female students but frequently depended on female instructors, even before the initial Philadelphia Sunday school of 1838. The public bat mitzvah ceremony, introduced by Mordecai Kaplan, resonated ultimately in modern Orthodox as well as in liberal Jewish settings and owed much to the reality that the Jewish education for girls was, with the exception of gender-separate Orthodox education in the traditional yeshiva sector, much the same as for boys.

Perennial challenges in Jewish education in America include personnel recruitment, training, and retention. The essential need for personnel had, by the end of the twentieth century, stimulated a proliferation of fellowship and in-service programs that prepare new recruits and strengthen the skills of those already in the field. The remuneration of Jewish educational professionals at levels that would attract and retain highly qualified personnel remained an insufficiently addressed concern.

The cost of providing and accessing the ever-expanding array of Jewish educational opportunities was another critical issue at the close of the twentieth century. Having developed such outstanding—and costly—frameworks as day schools and residential camps, the need for ensuring student access was compelling. If seats or beds, as the case may be, cost thousands of dollars per child per session, what was to be the standing of the majority of American Jews, unable to sustain the costs involved? The engagement of more private foundations in the cause of Jewish education and the example of the Birthright Israel program represented promising prospects, but the challenge of financial access to Jewish education remained considerable.

In 1918, Alexander Dushkin noted that American Jews placed charity at the center of their communal activity. Charity, though, is not "reproductive," he observed: "It does not guarantee in any way that the children of the Jewish philanthropists will continue to support or to be interested in Jewish charities. On the other hand, education is essentially reproductive, for it means the transmission of interests to the next generation. With education at the center of communal life, charity and all other communal activities inevitably follow. With charity at the center of communal life, not even the continuation of Jewish charity is assured."[360] By the close of the twentieth century, Jewish Federations and philanthropists were moving in the direction urged by Dushkin three generations earlier.

Results and Implications of the National Jewish Population Survey, 2000–2001

Results of the 2000–2001 National Jewish Population Survey (NJPS) suggested that, at the close of the twentieth century, the proverbial glass was both half full and half empty. Jewish population in the United States, estimated at 5.5 million by the 1990 NJPS, had declined to 5.2 million, 2 percent of the American population. The proportion of children was declining, and 19 percent of Jews were sixty-five years or older, as compared with 17 percent in 1990, and 12 percent for the United States general population. Indeed, the median age of the Jewish population had by 2000–2001 risen to forty-two, five years above the median age in 1990, and seven years older than the median age of the United States population as a whole.[361] These data were reminiscent of findings relating to acculturated American Jews of German extraction at the beginning of the twentieth century. Prospects for new waves of Jewish immigration were, in contrast to a hundred years earlier, virtually inconceivable. Based on the evidence, the NJPS pronounced unequivocally that "current Jewish fertility (below 1.9 per Jewish woman) will contribute over time to a declining Jewish population, if other sources of population growth such as immigration do not compensate for it."[362]

Consistent with the trend toward individualism in Jewish identity, the National Jewish Population Survey pointed to weakening ties among Jews on multiple levels, including friendship patterns, contributions to Jewish philanthropy, and attachment to Israel.[363] By 2001, 31 percent of all married Jews were intermarried, with the rate of intermarriage ranging from 13 percent among those married before 1970 to 47 percent among those married between 1996 and 2001.[364] For the first time, the NJPS indicated that among those aged six to seventeen receiving Jewish education, a plurality was educated in Jewish day schools / yeshivas (29 percent attended day school / yeshiva, 24 percent of students were enrolled in part-time—more than once a week—Jewish schools; 25 percent participated in one-day-a-week programs).[365] Moreover, among college and graduate students surveyed, 41 percent reported having taken a Jewish studies class as part of their course work to date.[366]

Analyzing the findings of the survey, sociologist Steven Cohen concluded: "[W]hile the overall Jewish population is bound to shrink, and while average levels of ethnic engagement are clearly bound to decline, the size and resources of the most heavily engaged Jewish population is just as likely to expand. The committed core of the million or so most active and educated Jews who have been responsible for building and sustaining Jewish institutional, cultural and political life in the past figures to retain or expand its numbers, and match or exceed its predecessors in commitment and educational preparation."[367] Though Jewish population was declining and many Jews lacked rudimentary Jewish education or more than an ephemeral sense of Jewish identity, the percentage of American Jews involved in serious Jewish study had never been greater, a circumstance that seemed to augur well for the future of American Jewry.

Salo Baron, the eminent Jewish historian of the twentieth century, stated: "If someone were to guarantee that, in the next generation

American Jews will harbor one hundred truly first-rate scholars, one hundred first-rate writers and rabbis, one hundred first-rate communal executives, and one hundred first-rate lay leaders—the total number would not exceed five hundred persons; a negligible and statistically hardly recognizable segment of the Jewish population—one could look forward confidently to American Judaism's reaching new heights of achievement."[368] Although it may have taken fifty years to arrive at Baron's prescription, American Jewry has, arguably, developed the requisite hundreds. First-rate Jewish leaders—lay and professional—nurtured by the Jewish educational opportunities of the latter half of the twentieth century, are making their mark in creating new and richer Jewish educational opportunities for adults and children in the twenty-first century. There is escalating investment in Jewish education on the part of Federations and major philanthropists and considerable movement from "pediatric," or pre–bar/bat mitzvah, Jewish education, toward lifelong Jewish learning. The dividends, which Baron projected might be realized from the hundreds, are today in evidence. The continuing vitality of Jewish life in the United States, its next steps in generations to come as in generations past, will surely owe much to the efforts of those who labor to "teach them diligently."

CHAPTER SEVEN
Into the Twenty-First Century

Though there may be some truth to the observation that Jews often incline to see the darkness at the end of the light—the late Jewish thinker Simon Rawidowicz famously noted that "there was hardly a generation in the Diaspora that did not consider itself the final link in Israel's chain"[369]—there is cause for optimism in developments in Jewish education in the United States early in the twenty-first century. Two hundred years ago, the Jewish education of successive generations of children in the United States was seen almost exclusively as a family concern. There has been substantial movement toward an ethos of Jewish communal responsibility for making Jewish education more widely available. The Birthright Israel program, recent community initiatives to develop endowments to secure the financial future of day schools, and the investments of mega-philanthropists as well as Jewish Federations in Jewish education reflect continuing movement toward the provision of Jewish education as a communal concern.

Jewish education, largely relegated to children at mid-twentieth century, had by the late twentieth century engaged more adult learners, and this trend continues early in the twenty-first century. Indeed, as the Jewish population ages, many Jewish-themed Elderhostel programs have developed, and additional programs of Jewish education targeted to seniors can be anticipated. Not only has expanded adult Jewish learning created more literate adult Jews; it has nurtured greater advocacy for the importance of Jewish education and created households in which children come to view their own Jewish educational pursuits as having adult significance.

There has been, as well, a broadening of the range of Jewish educational opportunities: day schools and congregational supplementary

119

schools; public and nonsectarian private high school Jewish clubs and service learning—Jewish learning and reflection tied to community service—models for youth; online study at many levels; *havurot* for adults and for families; and a variety of retreats and expanded residential camping opportunities and study seminars for all age cohorts. While it is too soon to fully grasp the long-term impact of September 11, 2001, on American life, the desire for community and search for meaning in a turbulent world may, for some, have strengthened their Jewish connection. Popular interest in kabbalah, Jewish mystical teachings, among Jews and non-Jews, may likewise be attributable to a quest for deeper understanding of enduring questions of meaning.

The early years of the new century saw many organizations working to transform American Jewish education. In 2003, PEJE announced a goal of doubling enrollment in other-than-Orthodox day schools over a ten-year period. In 2004, the Jewish Education Service of North America (JESNA) convened a summit on personnel in Jewish education and, in 2005, initiated a project—in collaboration with Bureaus of Jewish Education and religious movements with synagogues sponsoring afternoon schools—on coaching for change in congregational educational settings. CAJE, the Coalition for the Advancement of Jewish Education, drew national attention to the advancement of early childhood Jewish education. The Jewish Community Centers Association initiated programs to maximize the Jewish educational potential of early childhood, residential, and day camps. A number of initiatives, from the DeLeT (Day School Leadership through Teaching) program—a one-year induction program that trains college graduates to become day school teachers—to degree programs in Jewish education, trained educators for a field that was ripe for and open to innovation.

Congregational schools, still the primary venue of Jewish education for school-age children, experimented with a variety of models. Newer entries include avocational teachers (congregants with an interest in teaching) and home-based Hebrew tutoring—providing one-on-one instruction, ensuring 100 percent attendance, and enlisting parents in the educational process. Some congregations developed strategies for integrating their classroom-based and youth-group programs; others experimented with Shabbat programs, engaging parents and children in joint and parallel learning activities on a sustained basis.

Orthodoxy, which had pioneered the twentieth-century day school movement in the United States, faced a continuing conflict between traditional and integrationist yeshiva education. To what degree were general studies and Torah education two worlds—with general education viewed strictly in utilitarian terms? To what degree did these spheres of knowledge interact and inform each other? Inasmuch as the overwhelming number of yeshiva religious studies personnel were of traditional orientation—with roots and education in the traditional yeshiva (or women's seminary)—those schools whose boards and families inclined to an integrationist model found themselves, early in the twenty-first century, hard-pressed to enlist personnel to conduct schools committed to such an approach.

Bureaus of Jewish Education continued to play a role in linking their communities' schools and youth groups, offering continuing teacher education, facilitating vision and standard-setting within schools, disseminating best practices, and providing professional expertise in domains ranging from curriculum and instruction to governance and operations. Hebrew colleges, initially conceived as training grounds for educators who would teach in Talmud Torah schools, reengineered themselves and trained educators for an expanding range of professional roles, as well as training Jewish communal workers and mounting adult education initiatives for the Jewish community. As the self was clearly sovereign in the United States, so was the autonomy of each institution a well-established reality. Local bureaus and colleges as well as national organizations recognized that their worth lay in the ability to deliver something of perceived value, not in any notion of top-down hierarchy.

The role of individual philanthropists and foundations in driving Jewish educational activity presented the potential downside of highly idiosyncratic outcomes. Many foundations and mega-philanthropists, however, engaged Jewish educational professionals to serve of counsel and participated in a funders' network fostering broadened perspectives as to the state of the field and nurturing joint projects. Though there are, to be sure, divergent emphases, it has become clear to most policy makers and investors that there is no "one size fits all" approach to the provision of Jewish education.

Financial access to Jewish educational opportunity remains critical, particularly with regard to making day school education available to all who seek it. Although a Birthright Israel experience might cost a few thousand dollars per participant, it is a one-time communal cost. Day school, kindergarten through twelfth grade, for one student can cost $200,000; little has been done to address the challenge. Many in the yeshiva sector are vigorous advocates of government vouchers in support of private education, seeing such funds as a vital desideratum for the future of day school education. Such an approach has critics on multiple bases, ranging from concern about church-state separation, to concern for negative impact on educational opportunity for students not in Jewish day schools in a redistribution of funds from the prevailing model, to questions about the extent to which vouchers would actually make day school education more broadly accessible.

At the beginning of the twenty-first century, Jewish education occupies a prominent place among communal priorities, but the history of communal agenda setting is filled with shifting priorities. Pressing crises of social welfare, rising anti-Semitism, rescue of Jews threatened in other lands, or support of an embattled State of Israel can potentially displace Jewish education as a primary focus of communal attention and investment. Moreover, the history of education is replete with instances of failed expectations leading to "disillusionment and to blaming the schools for not solving problems beyond their reach."[370] Yet the proposition that the provision of Jewish educational opportunity is a matter for collective Jewish responsibility—for those who elect to become part of a collective—seems to have become integral to American Jewish life.

The articulation of a vision for Jewish living will be an enduring challenge in American Jewish education. At the beginning of the twenty-first century, it is comfortable to be Jewish in the United States. As Jews continue to shrink as a percentage of the population, and potentially are less favorably viewed in the public eye, maintaining a Jewish lifestyle will require, in each generation, compelling rationales. In a nation built on individualism, Jewish education is, for most people, a matter of personal choice. That more American Jewish students are enrolled in day schools (data released in 2005 showed enrollment growth from 185,000 students in 1998–99 to 205,000 students in 2003–04)[371] or that early education Hebrew language immersion programs are in vogue in some communities is not driven—for many who elect to participate in these programs—by a calculus of the impact of such choices on Jewish continuity, but on how the experience will benefit the learners' education, enabling them to lead a successful life in America. The recent popularity of Hebrew immersion in early childhood education is, in no small measure, driven by research indicating that acquisition of a second language early on can have significant learning benefits in other disciplines.

The coalescence of individual interests and the needs of the Jewish collective have frequently translated into a strengthening of Jewish life on both the personal and communal levels. The Talmudic sages recognized that actions undertaken with a narrow aim might have unintended, broader positive consequences. Many are the families whose ambivalent initial encounter with Jewish education has, through the positive experiences of their children, given way to more substantial, continuing engagement with Jewish learning. Early in the twentieth century, Jewish children attended public schools as an Americanizing activity; early in the twenty-first century, the Jewish school experiences of the descendants of those immigrant ancestors sometimes serve a Judaizing function, extending not only to the immediate learner but to students' homes.

A vision for those who promote Jewish educational opportunities for Jews in America was well articulated by the late Harvard University professor Isadore Twersky: "Our goal," he said, "should be to make it possible for every Jewish person, child or adult, to be exposed to the mystery and romance of Jewish history, to the enthralling insights and special sensitivities of Jewish thought, to the sanctity and symbolism of Jewish existence, and to the power and profundity of Jewish faith."[372] It is reasonable to project that the enduring vitality of American Jewry—living as Jews—will be closely associated with the degree to which this goal is achieved in the twenty-first century and beyond.

Notes

1. Jonathan Sacks, *The Dignity of Difference* (London: Continuum, 2003), 135.
2. Quoted in *A History of the Jewish People*, ed. H. H. Ben-Sasson (Cambridge, Mass.: Harvard University Press, 1976), 522.
3. United Jewish Communities, National Jewish Population Survey 2000–2001, (September 2003), http://www.ujc.org/page.html?ArticleID=33650, 14.
4. Jack Wertheimer, *Talking Dollars and Sense about Jewish Education* (New York: Avi Chai Foundation, 2001), 7.
5. Michael Zeldin, "The Promise of Historical Inquiry: Nineteenth-Century Jewish Day Schools and Twentieth-Century Policy," American Jewish Archives Small Collections–13885 (Los Angeles, 1987), 2.
6. Eduardo Rauch, *The Education of Jews and the American Community: 1840 to the New Millennium* (Tel Aviv: Tel Aviv University, 2004).
7. Judah Pilch, ed., *A History of Jewish Education in America* (New York: American Association for Jewish Education, 1969).
8. Lloyd Gartner, ed., *Jewish Education in the United States: A Documentary History* (New York: Teachers College Press, 1969).
9. Jonathan D. Sarna, "American Jewish Education in Historical Perspective," *Jewish Education* 64, nos. 1–2 (winter/spring 1998): 19.
10. Idem, *American Judaism* (New Haven, Conn.: Yale University Press, 2004).
11. Jonathan B. Krasner, "Representations of Self and Other in American Jewish History and Social Studies School Books: An Exploration of the Changing Shape of American Jewish Identity" (Ph.D. diss., Brandeis University, 2002).
12. Krasner's work concentrates on the mainstream, to the exclusion of textbooks used by the traditional Orthodox and the Yiddishists. He observes that for much of the period of his treatment, these groups utilized textbooks written primarily in Europe (ibid., 440). A recent contribution to the study of educational curricula designed for children focuses on texts developed for the teaching of Bible—"Bible stories"—from the early twentieth century to the close of the century. Penny Schine Gold, *Making the Bible Modern* (Ithaca, N.Y.: Cornell University Press, 2004).

13. Norman Drachler, *A Bibliography of Jewish Education in the United States* (Detroit: Wayne State University Press, 1996), xii.

14. Lawrence A. Cremin, *Traditions of American Education* (New York: Basic Books, 1977), viii.

15. Harold S. Himmelfarb, "The Impact of Religious Schooling: The Effects of Jewish Education Upon Adult Religious Involvement" (Ph.D. diss., University of Chicago, 1975); and Geoffrey F. Bock, "The Jewish Schooling of American Jews: A Study of Non-Cognitive Educational Effects" (Ph.D. diss., Harvard University, 1976).

16. Charles Liebman, *The Ambivalent American Jew* (Philadelphia: Jewish Publication Society, 1973).

17. Each such congregation was a synagogue-community—*kehal kodesh* (holy community)—"an all-embracing institution that both controlled every aspect of Jewish life and commanded allegiance from every Jew dwelling or sojourning within its ambit. . . . It promoted group solidarity and discipline, evoked a sense of tradition as well as a feeling of kinship toward similarly organized synagogue-communities throughout the Jewish world, and enhanced the chances that even small clusters of Jews, remote from the well-springs of Jewish learning, could survive from one generation to the next." Jonathan D. Sarna, "From Synagogue-Community to Community of Synagogues: A Turning Point in American History" (Brandeis University, 1990). Such sanctions as fines, loss of synagogue honors, and denial of burial rights became less and less effective over time, and the synagogue-community eroded in the early nineteenth century. Synagogues came to represent diversity rather than unity in American Jewish life. See Sarna, "From Synagogue-Community to Community of Synagogues"; and Leon Jick, *The Americanization of the Synagogue, 1820–1870* (Hanover, N.H.: Brandeis University Press, 1992).

18. See Marc D. Angel, "The Sephardim of the United States: An Exploratory Study," *American Jewish Year Book* 74 (1973): 77–138. While the homeland of these immigrants had, at one time, been Spain or Portugal, they had since moved on to the Netherlands or England. It is estimated that, in 1700, the Jewish population of the colonies numbered 250. Jacob R. Marcus, "The American Colonial Jew: A Study in Acculturation," in *The American Jewish Experience,* ed. Jonathan D. Sarna (New York: Holmes and Meier, 1997), 7. Trade and family ties reinforced connections among the scattered Sephardi colonists.

19. Marcus, "The American Colonial Jew," 13–14. An interesting case of a Jew actively involved in congregational life, desirous of maintaining the Jewish status of his household, is reflected in the following inquiry posed to the London Beth Din by the leadership of Philadelphia's Mikveh Israel in 1793:

> A (*Yehid*) of this Congregation has Lived in a Public way with a (*Goyeh*) woman who has Kept (House) for him about (eig)ht Years and has had By her three Children two of which are boys which he had (*Ge-mulim*)

at the 8th day, the Same Person *now* applies to us with the Consent of the Woman to make her a (*g-yo-reth*) as also grant him Permission to marry Said woman with (*Chupuh u-kidushim*).

We must Say in favor of the above (*Yehid*) that he has and does Keep up as far as we know to our Rules; and Contributes toward the support of our Congregation. As others do. We have represented to the best of our Knowledge the Case and Conduct of the person. and therefore request your opinion on the Subject and what we have to do.

Joseph L. Blau and Salo W. Baron, eds., *The Jews of the United States 1790–1840: A Documentary History* (New York: Columbia University Press, 1963), 2:589. This case reflects the reality that many Jewish immigrants were single men, and relationships with Christian women were not uncommon. As Marcus notes, in the remote areas a more typical consequence was marriage to a Christian and child-rearing in the mother's faith. In the absence of local rabbinic scholars, halakhic (Jewish legal) inquiries were, in the early decades of the American Republic, sent by Sephardim to London's Bevis Marks Synagogue and by Ashkenazim to British chief rabbi (1802–42) Solomon Hirschel. Lance J. Sussman, "Jewish Intellectual Activity and Educational Practice in the United States: 1776–1840," American Jewish Archives Small Collections–12167 (Cincinnati, 1978).

20. Sarna, *American Judaism*, 45.

21. The first ordained (Orthodox) rabbi to settle in the United States, Abraham Rice (1840), spent a frustrating period in the pulpit in Baltimore, eventually leaving his post to open a dry-goods store. He allegedly declared: "I do not want to have anything to do with Jews." Jacob R. Marcus, *The American Jew: 1585–1990* (Brooklyn, N.Y.: Carlson, 1995), 95. A sympathetic biography of Rice has been written by I. Harold Sharfman, *The First Rabbi* (Malibu, Calif.: Pangloss, 1988).

22. Jacob Kabakoff, "The Use of Hebrew by American Jews During the Colonial Period," in *Hebrew and the Bible in America: The First Two Centuries*, ed. Shalom Goldman (Hanover, N.H.: University Press of New England, 1993), 195.

23. Quoted in Jick, *The Americanization of the Synagogue*, 8.

24. Abraham Karp, *Jewish Continuity in America* (Tuscaloosa: University of Alabama Press, 1998), 18–19.

25. Edwin Wolf and Maxwell Whiteman, *History of the Jews of Philadelphia* (Philadelphia: Jewish Publication Society, 1957), 141.

26. For a biographical sketch of Seixas, see Jacob R. Marcus, *The Handsome Young Priest in the Black Gown* (Cincinnati: American Jewish Archives, 1970).

27. Doniel Zvi Kramer, *The Day Schools and Torah Umesorah* (New York: Yeshiva University Press, 1984), 4. The minute book of Congregation Shearith Israel notes that "on the 21st of Nisan, the seventh day of Pesach (1731), the

day of completing the first year at the Synagogue, there was made *codez* [concentrated] the *Yeshiba* called *Minhat Arab*." Alexander Dushkin, *Jewish Education in New York City* (New York: Bureau of Jewish Education, 1918), 449.

28. See (undated) History of Shearith Israel, Archives of the American Jewish Historical Society (New York), I-4, Box 1, in connection with the establishment of the Polonies Talmud Torah; and Blau and Baron, *The Jews of the United States 1790–1840*, 2:445–46, for the text of the school's petition for public funds.

29. See Jonathan D. Sarna, "The Jewish Experience in American Public and Private Education," in *Vouchers for School Choice: Challenge or Opportunity?*, ed. Marshall J. Breger and David M. Gordis (Boston: Wilstein Institute of Jewish Policy Studies, 1998), 131–36. The petition of Congregation Shearith Israel to the legislature of the state of New York to maintain state aid to religious schools (1813) is reprinted in *Religion and State in the American Jewish Experience*, ed. Jonathan D. Sarna and David G. Dalin (Notre Dame, Ind.: University of Notre Dame Press, 1997), 86–88. The original can be found in the archives of the American Jewish Historical Society, Lyons Collection, P-15, Box 13.

30. Archives of the American Jewish Historical Society, Lyons Collection, P-15, Box 2.

31. Ibid.

32. Ibid., roster of March 8, 1795.

33. Carvalho, a pioneer American Jewish educator, published a text called "A Key to the Hebrew Tongue," for instructional purposes. The thirty-two-page pamphlet included the letters of the Hebrew alphabet with different vowels accompanying them. Isolated Hebrew words and their English translations, and verses and portions of verses from the Bible with their English translations, constitute the majority of the work. The closing section of the publication presents the grammar of the Hebrew language. Carvalho's text was primarily written for adults—including Christians—studying the language. Benjamin L. Yapko, "Jewish Elementary Education in the United States: Colonial Period to 1900" (Ph.D. diss., American University, 1958), 111–12. Not until 1893 was there to be a school established (Gratz College) under Jewish auspices especially for the training of teachers. Julius Greenstone, "Jewish Education in the United States," *American Jewish Year Book* 16 (1914–15): 104–5.

34. Archives of the American Jewish Historical Society, Lyons Collection, P-15, Box 13.

35. Jacob Hartstein, "The Polonies Talmud Torah of New York," *Publications of the American Jewish Historical Society* 34 (1937): 130.

36. Eli Faber, "The Formative Era of American Jewish History," *American Jewish History* 86, no. 1 (autumn 1993): 20. On the Jews of Charleston, see Charles Reznikoff, *The Jews of Charleston* (Philadelphia: Jewish Publication Society, 1950); and James William Hagy, *This Happy Land: The Jews of Colonial and Antebellum Charleston* (Tuscaloosa: University of Alabama Press, 1993).

37. Saul Jacob Rubin, *Third to None: The Saga of Savannah Jewry* (Savannah, Ga.: Mickve Israel, 1983), 112.

38. Wolf and Whiteman, *History of the Jews of Philadelphia,* 132.

39. Sussman, "Jewish Intellectual Activity," 17.

40. Arthur Hertzberg, *The Jews in America: Four Centuries of an Uneasy Encounter* (New York: Simon and Schuster, 1989), 56.

41. Abraham J. Karp, *A History of the Jews in America* (Northvale, N.J.: J. Aronson, 1997), 23–24.

42. Ibid., 24.

43. In addition to the five colonial congregations, Richmond Jewry established a congregation in 1791.

44. Jacob R. Marcus, *United States Jewry, 1776–1985* (Detroit: Wayne State University Press, 1989), 390.

45. Jick, *The Americanization of the Synagogue,* 62.

46. Jonathan D. Sarna, "The Cyclical History of Adult Jewish Learning in the United States: Peers' Law and Its Implications," in *Educational Deliberations: Studies in Education Dedicated to Shlomo (Seymour) Fox,* ed. Mordecai Nisan and Oded Schremer (Jerusalem: Keter, 2005), 213.

47. Dianne Ashton, *Rebecca Gratz: Women and Judaism in Antebellum America* (Detroit: Wayne State University Press, 1997), 152.

48. Ibid., 145.

49. For an excellent biography of Isaac Leeser, see Lance Sussman, *Isaac Leeser and the Making of American Judaism* (Detroit: Wayne State University Press, 1995).

50. Wolf and Whiteman, *History of the Jews of Philadelphia,* 376–77.

51. Blau and Baron, *The Jews of the United States 1790–1840,* 2:448–49.

52. Ibid., 2:449.

53. "Rosa Mordecai's Recollection of the First Hebrew Sunday School," in *The Jew in the American World,* ed. Jacob R. Marcus (Detroit: Wayne State University Press, 1996), 153–54.

54. Ashton, *Rebecca Gratz,* 161.

55. Avraham Barkai, *Branching Out: German-Jewish Immigration to the United States, 1820–1914* (New York: Holmes and Meier, 1994), 103; and Yapko, "Jewish Elementary Education in the United States," 78.

56. Quoted in Myron Berman, *Richmond's Jewry* (Charlottesville: University of Virginia Press, 1979), 56.

57. Melissa Klapper, "'A Fair Portion of the World's Knowledge': Jewish Girls Coming of Age in America, 1860–1920" (Ph.D. diss., Rutgers University, 2001), 240.

58. Isaac Leeser, *Catechism for Younger Children: Designed as a Religious Manual for House and School* (Philadelphia: Sherman, 1839), vi. On the writing of catechisms in Western Europe during the nineteenth century, see Jacob J. Petuchowski, "Manuals and Catechisms of the Jewish Religion in the Early Period

of Emancipation," in *Studies in Nineteenth-Century Jewish Intellectual History*, ed. Alexander Altmann (Cambridge, Mass.: Harvard University Press, 1964), 47–64.

59. Leeser, *Catechism for Younger Children*, 1.
60. Idem, *The Hebrew Reader: Designed as an Easy Guide to the Hebrew Tongue, for Jewish Children and Self-Instruction* (Philadelphia: Sherman, 1838).
61. Ibid., 4th ed. (1856).
62. Sarna, "The Cyclical History of Adult Jewish Learning in the United States," 211.
63. Isaac Leeser, " 'The Testimony': An Address Delivered Nisan 5611" (Philadelphia, 1851).
64. Idem, "Jewish Children under Gentile Teachers," in *The Occident* 1 (1843): 411.
65. Idem, *Discourses* X (Philadelphia, 1867): 140–41.
66. Idem, *Discourses* III (Philadelphia, 1841): 310–11.
67. Idem, "Jewish Children under Gentile Teachers," 413.
68. Idem, *Discourses* III, 320.
69. Idem, "A Plea for Education," *The Occident* 4 (1846): 114.
70. Hasia R. Diner, *The Jews of the United States, 1654–2000* (Berkeley: University of California Press, 2004), 80.
71. Paul S. Boyer et al., *The Enduring Vision* (Lexington, Mass.: D. C. Heath, 1996), 1:400.
72. Hasia R. Diner and Beryl Lieff Benderly, *Her Works Praise Her: A History of Jewish Women in America from Colonial Times to the Present* (New York: Basic Books, 2002), 86.
73. Naomi W. Cohen, *Encounter with Emancipation: The German Jews in the United States 1830–1914* (Philadelphia: Jewish Publication Society, 1984), 39.
74. Isaac Mayer Wise, "The New American Jew: American Jewish Life as Seen from Albany, New York, September 1847," trans. (from German) Sefton D. Temkin (Albany, N.Y.: Congregation Beth Emeth, 1977). Wise had received some yeshiva training and the equivalent of gymnasium education. For information on the life and thought of Isaac Mayer Wise, see James G. Heller, *Isaac M. Wise* (New York: Union of American Hebrew Congregations, 1965); and Sefton D. Temkin, *Isaac Mayer Wise* (Oxford: Oxford University Press, 1992).
75. Wise, "The New American Jew." Though, in this early analysis, Wise promoted the day school—indeed, he established one in Albany—he was later to become a proponent of Sunday schools.
76. Leeser, "A Plea for Education," 64.
77. "Objects and Means of Religious Education," *The Occident* 2 (1844): 193. Authorship of the article is ascribed to J. K. G. of Boston.
78. Henry Illoway, *Sefer Milkhamot Elohim: The Controversial Letters and the Casuistic Decisions of the Late Rabbi Bernard Illowy, Ph.D.* (Berlin: M. Poppelauer, 1914), 16–17.

79. Hyman Grinstein, *The Rise of the Jewish Community of New York, 1654–1860* (Philadelphia: Jewish Publication Society, 1947), 564 n. 27.

80. Alvin Schiff, *The Jewish Day School in America* (New York: Jewish Education Committee Press, 1966), 25–26; and Eduardo L. Rauch, "Jewish Education in the United States: 1840–1920" (Ed.D. diss., Harvard University, 1978), 49. For lists of and newspaper references to the many Jewish day schools and boarding schools functioning in the 1850s and 1860s, see Floyd S. Fierman, *Sources of Jewish Education in America Prior to 1881* (El Paso, Tex., 1960), 130–40.

81. Schiff, *The Jewish Day School in America*, 25. Hebrew language study in these schools "began with the Hebrew alphabet, then moved on to syllables and words in the *Siddur* (the daily and Sabbath prayer book), and then to Pentateuch translation. Occasionally, Hebrew writing was added." Alvin Schiff, *The Mystique of Hebrew: An Ancient Language in the New World* (New York: Shengold, 1996), 61.

82. Zeldin, "The Promise of Historical Inquiry," 9.

83. Among the finest of these private schools was the one in New York operated by Max Lilienthal. See Hyman Grinstein, "In the Course of the Nineteenth Century," in *A History of Jewish Education in America*, ed. Pilch, 39.

84. Diner, *The Jews of the United States*, 143.

85. Jacob R. Marcus, ed., *The American Jewish Woman: A Documentary History* (New York: Ktav, 1981), 173.

86. Sarna, "The Cyclical History of Adult Jewish Learning in the United States," 213.

87. Abraham P. Gannes, ed., *Selected Writings of Leo L. Honor* (New York: Reconstructionist Press, 1965), 36. For a history of YMHAs, see Benjamin Rabinowitz, *The Young Men's Hebrew Associations, 1854–1913* (New York: National Jewish Welfare Board, 1948).

88. Shuly Rubin Schwartz, *The Emergence of Jewish Scholarship in America* (Cincinnati: Hebrew Union College Press, 1991), 11.

89. Though much attention has been accorded German Jewish immigration, there is cause to consider the "English factor" in the shaping of American Judaism. Isaac Leeser consulted and sometimes reprinted—with attribution—Anglo-Jewish works in his publishing ventures. Samuel Meyer Isaacs, a Dutch-born Jew who spent many years in England, was among the key organizers of the Board of Delegates of American Israelites (1859), modeled after the Board of Deputies of British Jews. Morris Jacob Raphall (who occupied the pulpit of B'nai Jeshurun in New York), the most renowned English-speaking orator of mid-nineteenth-century America, came to the U.S. by way of a pulpit in Birmingham, England; he brought the enlightened Orthodoxy then developing in England to his new setting. Sabato Morais, who served Mikveh Israel in Philadelphia, 1851–97, came to the U.S. after five years of service in London. Indeed, in a recent work, David Ruderman suggests that "historians pay more attention to the impact of the Anglo-Jewish paradigm, of being Jewish in an

English key, on the fashioning of an American Jewish culture. [A] rethinking of the Anglo-Jewish connection seems called for." David B. Ruderman, *Jewish Enlightenment in an English Key* (Princeton, N.J.: Princeton University Press, 2000), 273.

90. Grinstein, "In the Course of the Nineteenth Century," 49.

91. Walter Ehrlich, *Zion in the Valley: The Jewish Community of St. Louis* (Columbia: University of Missouri Press, 2002), 133.

92. Article by B. A. Abrams, in Gartner, *Jewish Education in the United States,* 99–100.

93. Quoted in Marc Lee Raphael, *Profiles in American Judaism* (San Francisco: Harper and Row, 1984), 131.

94. Jick, *The Americanization of the Synagogue,* 71.

95. See Reznikoff, *The Jews of Charleston,* 126–41.

96. Michael A. Meyer, "America: The Reform Movement's Land of Promise," in *The American Jewish Experience,* ed. Sarna, 61.

97. For a biographical sketch of David Einhorn, see Kaufmann Kohler, "A Biographical Essay," in *David Einhorn Memorial Volume,* ed. idem (New York: Bloch, 1911), 403–55.

98. David Einhorn, "Inaugural Sermon," trans. C. A. Rubenstein (Baltimore, 1909), 15–16.

99. Leeser's journal was known overseas as the voice of American Jewish traditionalism. The Archives of the American Jewish Historical Society (P-20) include a letter to Leeser from Dr. Mendel Hirsch, son of Samson Raphael Hirsch, who served as dean of the (Orthodox) Samson Raphael Hirsch Real Schule in Frankfurt am Main. The letter, dated January 5, 1858, indicates that Dr. Hirsch had been approached by a number of English families regarding enrollment of their children at the school and proposes that Leeser promote the institution in *The Occident.*

100. The Board of Delegates was established in response to the Mortara Affair, the case in Rome of an abducted, baptized Jewish child seized—and retained—by papal authorities. Jews in the United States, as elsewhere, lobbied unsuccessfully to reunite the Mortara family. Records of the Board of Delegates of American Israelites can be found in the Archives of the American Jewish Historical Society, I-2.

101. Grinstein, "In the Course of the Nineteenth Century," 42–44.

102. Quoted in David Ellenson, "A Jewish Legal Decision by Rabbi Bernard Illowy of New Orleans and Its Discussion in Nineteenth-Century Europe," in idem, *Tradition in Transition* (Lanham, Md.: University Press of America, 1989), 105–6.

103. Isaac M. Wise, "Propositions Submitted to the Gentlemen of the Commission Appointed by the Council of the Union of American Hebrew Congregations at Milwaukee, July 11, 1878." Quoted in David Ellenson and Lee Bycel, "A Seminary of Sacred Learning," in *Tradition Renewed: A History of the Jewish*

Theological Seminary of America, ed. Jack Wertheimer (New York: Jewish Theological Seminary, 1997), 2:531.

104. With regard to the immigrants' interest in the preservation of German culture, public schools in some areas of high German immigrant population included German in their curricular offerings. Indeed, German Jews were among the German language teaching corps.

105. U.S. Commissioner of Education, Report, 1870 (Washington, D.C., 1875), 370, quoted in Gartner, *Jewish Education in the United States,* 86.

106. Bernard Felsenthal, "Jüdisches Schulwesen in America" (Chicago, 1866), excerpted and translated in Gartner, *Jewish Education in the United States,* 83–84. Felsenthal authored two Hebrew language textbooks. Schiff, *The Mystique of Hebrew,* 47.

107. Lloyd Gartner, "Temples of Liberty Unpolluted: American Jews and Public Schools," in *A Bicentennial Festschrift for Jacob Rader Marcus,* ed. Bertram W. Korn (New York: Ktav, 1976), 166.

108. Schiff, *The Jewish Day School in America,* 27.

109. N. Cohen, *Encounter with Emancipation,* 92.

110. Morton Merowitz, "Max Lilienthal (1814–1882): Jewish Educator in Nineteenth-Century America," *YIVO Annual of Jewish Social Science* 15 (1974): 57. The name of the magazine was changed to *The Sabbath School Visitor* in 1879.

111. Ashton, *Rebecca Gratz,* 167.

112. Moses Mielziner, "Pedagogics in the Sabbath-School," in *Moses Mielziner,* ed. Ella McKenna Friend Mielziner (New York, 1931), 118.

113. Ibid., 120.

114. Ibid.

115. Isaac Mayer Wise, *Judaism: Its Doctrines and Duties* (Cincinnati: Published in the office of *The Israelite,* 1872), 4.

116. It is instructive to compare Wise's *The Essence of Judaism* (Cincinnati: Bloch, 1861) with its revised version (1872), *Judaism: Its Doctrines and Duties.* Though Wise had opted for the Sunday school framework for religious studies, his curricular expectations remained unchanged.

117. Wise, *Judaism: Its Doctrines and Duties,* 3–4.

118. Quoted in David deSola Pool, "George Washington and Religious Liberty" (New York, 1932), 4.

119. Rauch, "Jewish Education in the United States," 311.

120. Reprinted in Paul R. Mendes-Flohr and Jehuda Reinharz, eds., *The Jew in the Modern World* (New York: Oxford University Press, 1995), 475.

121. Quoted in N. Cohen, *Encounter with Emancipation,* 172.

122. William Toll, "From Domestic Judaism to Public Ritual: Women and Religious Identity in the American West," in *Women and American Judaism,* ed. Pamela S. Nadell and Jonathan D. Sarna (Hanover, N.H.: University Press of New England, 2001), 141.

123. See Jonathan D. Sarna, *A Great Awakening: The Transformation That Shaped Twentieth-Century American Judaism and Its Implications for Today* (New York: Council for Initiatives in Jewish Education, 1995).
124. Peggy Kronsberg Pearlstein, "Understanding through Education: One Hundred Years of the Jewish Chautauqua Society, 1893–1993" (Ph.D. diss., George Washington University, 1993), 23.
125. On Henry Berkowitz and the Jewish Chautauqua Society, see Max Berkowitz, *The Beloved Rabbi: An Account of the Life and Works of Henry Berkowitz* (New York: Macmillan, 1932).
126. Diana Hirschler, *Young Folks Reading Union* (Kansas City: Berkowitz, 1893), 4; quoted in Pearlstein, "Understanding through Education," 90.
127. In 1939, the Jewish Chautauqua Society merged into the National Federation of Temple Brotherhoods; the NFTB saw the university work of the society as an instrument for combating anti-Semitism. Sarna attributes the shift from adult Jewish learning to university lectures—primarily to non-Jews—to changing priorities and a lack of funds. As combating anti-Semitism became a top Jewish communal priority, funds could be more readily secured to sustain education associated with the battle against anti-Semitism than for the goal of advancing lifelong Jewish learning. Sarna, "The Cyclical History of Adult Jewish Leaning," 218.
128. Krasner, "Representations of Self and Other," 77.
129. Ibid., 64–65.
130. Ibid., 40. By the first decade of the twentieth century, examples of the Hebrew nationalist orientation that was to be popularized by Samson Benderly were also in evidence in several cities. Meir Ben-Horin, "From the Turn of the Century to the Late Thirties," in *A History of Jewish Education in America*, ed. Pilch, 63–67.
131. Ibid., 59.
132. Abraham P. Gannes, *Central Community Agencies for Jewish Education* (Philadelphia: Dropsie College, 1954), 2.
133. Moses Weinberger, *People Walk on Their Heads,* trans. and ed. Jonathan D. Sarna (New York: Holmes and Meier, 1982), 51–52.
134. On the founding of Yeshivat Etz Chaim, see Gilbert Klapperman, *The Story of Yeshiva University* (New York: Macmillan, 1969), 17–21.
135. Schiff, *The Jewish Day School in America,* 30.
136. Klapperman, *The Story of Yeshiva University,* 27.
137. Kramer, *The Day Schools and Torah Umesorah,* 4.
138. Klapperman, *The Story of Yeshiva University,* 52. On the founding and early years of RIETS, see ibid., 48–72.
139. Quoted in ibid., 49.
140. Ibid., 74.
141. Diner opines: "The transplantation to America of Eastern European orthodoxy probably played as great a role in galvanizing the Seminary . . . as did the

developments in Reform." Hasia R. Diner, "Like the Antelope and the Badger," in *Tradition Renewed,* ed. Wertheimer, 1:12.

142. For the text of the Pittsburgh Platform, setting forth classical Reform Judaism, see Michael A. Meyer and W. Gunther Plaut, eds., *The Reform Judaism Reader* (New York: Union of American Hebrew Congregations Press, 2001), 197–99. The Reform approach had serious implications for how Bible, for example, should be taught. As Rabbi Schreiber asked (rhetorically) at the 1890 gathering of the Central Conference of American Rabbis: "Shall the teacher . . . instruct the pupils in accord with the antiquated ideas on inspiration, miracles, divine authority of the Bible, revelation, thus ignoring or even defying the results of history, geology, biology and natural philosophy?" Emanuel Schreiber, "How to Teach Biblical History in Our Sabbath Schools," *CCAR Proceedings* 1 (1890–91): 59.

143. On the founding of the Jewish Theological Seminary, see Moshe Davis, *The Emergence of Conservative Judaism* (Philadelphia: Jewish Publication Society, 1963), 235–41. Drachman, Schneeberger, and Mendes were involved in the Orthodox Jewish Congregational Union of America (established in 1898), and JTS rabbis mentored the founders of Young Israel (1912), whose goal was the revival of Judaism among second-generation Eastern European Jews in America. Bernard Felsenthal, a Reform rabbinic leader in the United States for over four decades, expressed deep concern about the spiritual vitality of the Reform movement as it was developing in the United States. Kaufmann Kohler, author of the Pittsburgh Platform, had become president of HUC in 1903, and early-twentieth-century American Reform Judaism reflected the platform's principles. Writing to a colleague in 1907, Felsenthal commented: "It will, one day, be recognized that what we call 'Reform Judaism' is not the highest and finest and best thing to be found in modern devotion. The thought often comes to mind that this extreme Reform we have in America, which knows no limit, will lead gradually to the extinction of Israel and its religion." Emma Felsenthal, ed., *Bernard Felsenthal: Teacher in Israel* (New York: Oxford University Press, 1924), 94.

144. Ellenson and Bycel, "A Seminary of Sacred Learning," 528.

145. Arthur A. Goren, *Jews and the Quest for Community: The Kehilla Experiment* (New York: Columbia University Press, 1970), 23.

146. Mel Scult, "Schechter's Seminary," in *Tradition Renewed,* ed. Wertheimer, 76.

147. Klapperman, *The Story of Yeshiva University,* 102.

148. Ibid., 139.

149. David Kaufman, "Jewish Education as a Civilization," in *Tradition Renewed,* ed. Wertheimer, 1:578.

150. Sarna, "The Cyclical History of Adult Jewish Learning in the United States," 215.

151. Quoted in Goren, *Jews and the Quest for Community,* 25.

152. "First Community Survey of Jewish Education in New York City—1909," reprinted in *Jewish Education* 20, no. 3 (summer 1949): 113–14.

153. Ibid., 114.
154. Ibid.
155. Ibid., 115.
156. Ibid.
157. Ibid.
158. See Rauch, "Jewish Education in the United States," 392–411.
159. Benderly, "Letter of Samson Benderly to Judah Magnes, March 9, 1910," reprinted in *Jewish Education* 20, no. 3 (summer 1949): 111.
160. For a biography of Benderly's early years, see Nathan H. Winter, *Jewish Education in a Pluralist Society* (New York: New York University Press, 1966), 27–34.
161. Ibid., 43.
162. Ibid., 35.
163. Judah L. Magnes to mass meeting of Federation of American Zionists, July 3, 1910; Magnes Papers, File 534, quoted in Arthur A. Goren, "Spiritual Zionists and Jewish Sovereignty," in *The Americanization of the Jews,* ed. Robert M. Seltzer and Norman J. Cohen (New York: New York University Press, 1995), 168.
164. Ahad Ha'am, "The Jewish State and the Jewish Problem (1897)," in *The Zionist Idea,* ed. Arthur Hertzberg (Philadelphia: Jewish Publication Society, 1997), 267. For a superb biography of Ahad Ha'am and a rich discussion of his version of Zionism and its impact, see Steven J. Zipperstein, *Elusive Prophet: Ahad Ha'am and the Origins of Zionism* (Berkeley: University of California Press, 1993). Even as pioneers made their way to Palestine, many Hebrew-oriented, cultural Zionists landed in New York. A Hebrew-speaking society—Mefitzei Sefat Ever Vesifrutah (Promoters of the Hebrew Language and Its Literature)—was founded in New York City in 1902 (Schiff, *The Mystique of Hebrew,* 49). "Among the East European immigrants to the United States in the early 1900's were outstanding young Hebraic scholars who contributed significantly to Hebrew culture and Jewish life in America via their teachings and writings. These included among others: A. H. Friedland, founder of the *Bet HaSefer HaLeumi* (The National Hebrew School for Girls) in 1911; Israel Efros, university professor and poet who founded the Baltimore Hebrew College; Pinkhos Churgin, Hebrew educator, Bible scholar, and Zionist leader who served as dean of the Teachers Institute of Yeshiva University; Moshe Feinstein, Hebrew poet who headed the Herzliah Teachers Institute in New York; Ephraim Lisitzky, poet and educator who was principal of a model community supplementary school in New Orleans; Daniel Persky, journalist who dedicated his life to teaching Hebrew language and literature on the college level; Menachem Ribalow, essayist and longtime editor of *Hadoar;* and Eisig Silberschlag, poet and critic who was president of the Hebrew College in Boston" (Schiff, 53). On Hebrew culture in the U.S. in the first half of the twentieth century, see Alan Mintz, ed., *Hebrew in America* (Detroit: Wayne State University Press, 1993).

165. Louis Brandeis, "The Jewish Problem: How to Solve It," reprinted in Mendes-Flohr and Reinharz, *The Jew in the Modern World*, 496.

166. Despite his optimism about cultural nationalist Jewish education in the American environment, Benderly cautioned that in the lands outside of the Land of Israel, the Jewish people would "constantly suffer losses." Presentation to Achvah Club, November 26, 1910; quoted in Gartner, *Jewish Education in the United States*, 128.

167. Samson Benderly, "Jewish Education in America," *The Jewish Exponent*, January 17, 1908. Reprinted in *Jewish Education* 20, no. 3 (summer 1949): 82.

168. Ibid., 86.

169. Kaufman, "Jewish Education as a Civilization," 588.

170. Mel Scult, ed., *Communings of the Spirit: The Journals of Mordecai M. Kaplan, 1913–1934* (Detroit: Wayne State University Press, 2001), 77.

171. Kaufman, "Jewish Education as a Civilization," 583. It is interesting to note that girls' secondary school education was far greater among Jews than among any other immigrant group. "Foreign-born Jewish boys graduated high school at double the rate and foreign-born Jewish girls at triple the rate of any other immigrant group." Diner and Benderly, *Her Works Praise Her*, 221.

172. Shuly Rubin Schwartz, "Rebecca Aaronson Brickner: Preacher, Teacher, and Rebbetzin in Israel," *American Jewish Archives Journal* 54, no. 1 (2002): 65–66.

173. Scult, *Communings of the Spirit*, 76.

174. Kaufman, "Jewish Education as a Civilization," 598–601.

175. Karp, *A History of the Jews in America*, 237.

176. Zevi Scharfstein, *Arbaim shana be-Amerikah* (Tel Aviv: Masadah, 1956), 173. In general, administrative progressives of the era believed that educational governance was best left to professional leadership, and they disparaged lay control.

177. For a description and analysis of the writings and activities of five of the most prominent "Benderly boys"—Isaac Berkson, Samuel Dinin, Alexander Dushkin, Emanuel Gamoran, and Leo Honor—see Walter Ackerman, "The Americanization of Jewish Education," *Judaism* 24, no. 4 (1975): 416–35.

178. Quoted in Miriam Heller Stern, "A Dream Not Quite Come True: Reassessing the Benderly Era in Jewish Education," *Journal of Jewish Education* 70, no. 3 (fall 2004): 23.

179. "Report of the Special Committee on Religious Educational Societies," made to the Board of the New York Federation, March 12, 1917. Quoted in Gannes, *Central Community Agencies for Jewish Education*, 185–87.

180. Ibid., 187.

181. As the number and variety of Jewish educational entities outside the orbit of the bureau proliferated, a new umbrella agency for New York Jewish education, the Jewish Education Committee (JEC), was established. Launched in 1939, the committee was headed by Alexander Dushkin, one of the original

Benderly boys. In 1941, all remaining activities of the BJE were turned over to the JEC, and Benderly was retired on a pension.

182. Klapper, "'A Fair Portion of the World's Knowledge,'" 244.
183. Lewis S. Feuer, "The Golden Age of the Downtown Talmud Torah in New York's Lower East Side," unpublished memoir, American Jewish Archives Small Collections–13784, 14–16.
184. Walter I. Ackerman. "What We Know About Schools," in *What We Know About Jewish Education,* ed. Stuart L. Kelman (Los Angeles: Torah Aura, 1992), 27.
185. Diner, *The Jews of the United States,* 149.
186. Ackerman, "What We Know About Schools," 28.
187. Gartner, *Jewish Education in the United States,* 20. For a description of the various types of Yiddish schools, see Rauch, "Jewish Education in the United States," 451–56. It has been estimated that 600,000 people in the United States read the daily Yiddish press in 1915. Marcus, *The American Jew, 1585–1990,* 207.
188. Diner and Benderly, *Her Works Praise Her,* 230.
189. Kramer, *The Day Schools and Torah Umesorah,* 4.
190. Jenna Weissman Joselit, *New York's Jewish Jews: The Orthodox Community in the Interwar Years* (Bloomington: Indiana University Press, 1990), 133.
191. Schiff, *The Jewish Day School in America,* 44.
192. Kramer, *The Day Schools and Torah Umesorah,* 5.
193. Rauch, "Jewish Education in the United States," 346–50.
194. Sarna and Dalin, *Religion and State in the American Jewish Experience,* 205–6.
195. Ibid., 207.
196. Jonathan D. Sarna, "The Crucial Decade in Jewish Camping," in *A Place of Our Own: The Rise of Reform Jewish Camping,* ed. Michael M. Lorge and Gary P. Zola (Tuscaloosa: University of Alabama Press, 2006), 29.
197. Ben-Horin, "From the Turn of the Century to the Late Thirties," 100–104.
198. Sarna, "The Crucial Decade in Jewish Camping," 32–35.
199. Abraham P. Gannes and Levi Soshuk, "The Kvutzah and Camp Achvah," *Jewish Education* 20, no. 3 (summer 1949): 63. The important roles of drama, dance, and music at Achvah—as in all the educational settings that Benderly shaped—are considered in a series of reminiscences by those who worked closely with him in these domains: Samuel J. Citron, "Dr. Benderly's Love of Drama," *Jewish Education* 20, no. 3 (summer 1949): 70–74; Dvora Lapson, "An Intuitive Approach to the Dance," *Jewish Education* 20, no. 3 (summer 1949): 75–76; and Moshe Nathanson, "Dr. Benderly as Impresario," *Jewish Education* 20, no. 3 (summer 1949): 77–78.
200. BBYO (B'nai B'rith Youth Organization) was established in 1944, comprising AZA and BBG.
201. Stanley A. Ginsburgh, "A Study of Nationally Organized Jewish Youth Groups

in America as Educational Agencies for the Preservation of the Jewish Cultural Heritage," American Jewish Archives, Microfilm 74 (diss., Massachusetts State College, 1940), 22–25.

202. Gary P. Zola, "Jewish Camping and Its Relationship to the Organized Camping Movement in America," in *A Place of Our Own*, ed. Lorge and Zola, 15.

203. Ginsburgh, "A Study of Nationally Organized Jewish Youth Groups," 33.

204. Diner and Benderly, *Her Works Praise Her*, 222.

205. Ibid., 280.

206. Diner, *The Jews of the United States*, 226.

207. Ben-Horin, "From the Turn of the Century to the Late Thirties," 84. Enrollment in Hebrew teachers' colleges peaked in the 1950s, at about 3,000 students. From their inception until the 1960s, instruction in these institutions was in Hebrew. Schiff, *The Hebrew Mystique*, 64.

208. Isidor Margolis, *Jewish Teacher Training Schools in the United States* (New York: National Council for Torah Education of Mizrachi–Hapoel Hamizrachi, 1964), 193–210.

209. Greenstone, "Jewish Education in the United States," 124.

210. Ben-Horin, "From the Turn of the Century to the Late Thirties," 88–90.

211. AAJE was to be reconstituted as JESNA (Jewish Education Service of North America) in 1981. Jack Wertheimer, "Jewish Education in the United States: Recent Trends and Issues," *American Jewish Year Book* 99 (1999): 32.

212. Ben-Horin, "From the Turn of the Century to the Late Thirties," 110.

213. Preamble to the constitution of the United Synagogue, quoted in Elliot N. Dorff, *Conservative Judaism: Our Ancestors to Our Descendants* (New York: United Synagogue of America Youth Commission, 1977), 240.

214. Zevi Scharfstein, *History of Jewish Education* (Jerusalem: R. Mas, 1960), 3:79–80. Translation mine.

215. For a biography, including attention to the educational initiatives of Bernard Revel, see Aaron Rothkoff, *Bernard Revel: Builder of American Orthodoxy* (Philadelphia: Jewish Publication Society of America, 1972).

216. Ibid., 46.

217. Rabbi Joseph Soloveitchik arrived in the United States in 1932 and settled in Boston, which—despite his position in New York—remained his home until his death, in 1993. For a look at Rabbi Soloveitchik's impact on Boston Jewry—not the least of which was through his association with the Maimonides School—see Seth Farber, *An American Orthodox Dreamer* (Hanover, N.H.: University Press of New England, 2004).

218. Ellenson and Bycel, "A Seminary of Sacred Learning," 548.

219. See Ezra Spicehandler, "Hebrew Language and Literature at the Hebrew Union College–Jewish Institute of Religion, 1876–1930," in *Jewish Education and Learning*, ed. Glenda Abramson and Tudor Parfitt (Langhome, Pa.: Harwood Academic Publishers, 1994), 45.

220. Ellenson and Bycel, "A Seminary of Sacred Learning," 551.

221. Alan Silverstein, *Alternatives to Assimilation* (Hanover, N.H.: University Press of New England, 1994), 158.

222. On the refugee scholars project of the college, see Michael A. Meyer, *Judaism within Modernity* (Detroit: Wayne State University Press, 2001), 345–61.

223. Ellenson and Bycel, "A Seminary of Sacred Learning," 544–45.

224. Isaac B. Berkson and Ben Rosen, "Jewish Education Survey of Cleveland," *Jewish Education* 9, no. 1 (January–March 1937): 13.

225. Diner, *The Jews of the United States*, 228.

226. Ibid., 253.

227. The first coeducational yeshiva day school in the United States was Yeshiva of Flatbush, founded in 1928. Jeffrey S. Gurock, "The Ramaz Version of American Orthodoxy," in *RAMAZ: School, Community, Scholarship and Orthodoxy*, ed. idem (Hoboken, N.J.: Ktav, 1989), 49.

228. Quoted in ibid., 44–45.

229. Winter, *Jewish Education in a Pluralist Society*, 187.

230. David Tyack and Larry Cuban, *Tinkering toward Utopia: A Century of Public School Reform* (Cambridge, Mass.: Harvard University Press, 1995), 68.

231. Mordecai M. Kaplan, *Judaism as a Civilization: Toward a Reconstruction of American-Jewish Life*, new ed. (Philadelphia: Jewish Publication Society, 1994; 1st ed., 1934), 489–90.

232. Ibid., 216.

233. Krasner, "Representations of Self and Other," 136.

234. Ibid., 158, 167.

235. Emanuel Gamoran, "Recent Tendencies in Education and Their Application to the Jewish School," *CCAR Yearbook* 33 (1923): 317.

236. Lee Levinger, *A History of the Jews in the United States* (Cincinnati: Union of American Hebrew Congregations, 1930). Originally published in 1930, the book—by Levinger's death in 1966—had undergone four revisions, twenty editions, and numerous printings. Krasner, "Representations of Self and Other," 206.

237. Levinger, *A History of the Jews in the United States*, 406.

238. Mamie Gamoran, *Hillel's Happy Holidays* (Cincinnati: Union of American Hebrew Congregations, 1939), viii.

239. Michael A. Meyer, *Response to Modernity* (Detroit: Wayne State University Press, 1995), 301.

240. Leo Jung and Joseph Kaminetsky, eds., *A Model Program for the Talmud Torah* (New York: Union of Orthodox Jewish Congregations of America, 1942), 23.

241. Ibid., 31.

242. Ibid., 19.

243. Quoted in Kramer, *The Day Schools and Torah Umesorah*, 12–13.

244. Hertzberg, *The Jews in America*, 321.

245. Jack Wertheimer, "Recent Trends in American Judaism," *American Jewish Year Book* 89 (1989): 65.

246. Though less than 4 percent of the United States population, Jews constituted 8 percent of the nation's World War II military personnel. Diner and Benderly, *Her Works Praise Her,* 296.

247. Jack Wertheimer, "The Conservative Synagogue," in *The American Synagogue: A Sanctuary Transformed,* ed. idem (New York: Cambridge University Press, 1987), 125.

248. Hertzberg, *The Jews in America,* 323.

249. Quoted in William Helmreich, *The World of the Yeshiva* (Hoboken, N.J.: Ktav, 2000), 303.

250. Isa Aron, "From the Congregational School to the Learning Congregation," in *A Congregation of Learners,* ed. Isa Aron, Sara Lee, and Seymour Rossel (New York: Union of American Hebrew Congregations Press, 1995), 62.

251. Wertheimer, "Recent Trends in American Judaism," 66.

252. Judah Pilch, "From the Early Forties to the Mid-Sixties," in *A History of Jewish Education in America,* ed. idem, 130.

253. Ibid., 162–63.

254. Participation in high school education in general rose dramatically in America during the twentieth century. In 1900, one in ten Americans aged fourteen to seventeen was enrolled in high school. This figure rose, rapidly, to seven in ten, by 1940, and reached nine in ten by 1980. Tyack and Cuban, *Tinkering toward Utopia,* 47.

255. Simon Greenberg, "The Congregational School Three Days a Week," in *Jewish Schools in America* (New York: American Association for Jewish Education, 1946), 14–18.

256. Stuart Schoenfeld, "Folk Judaism, Elite Judaism and the Role of the Bar Mitzvah in the Development of the Synagogue and Jewish School in America," *Contemporary Jewry* 9 (1988): 73.

257. Ibid., 76.

258. Emanuel Gamoran, "The Jewish Sunday School," in *Jewish Schools in America* (New York: American Association for Jewish Education, 1946), 46–48.

259. Aron, "From the Congregational School to the Learning Congregation," 63.

260. Alexander Dushkin, *Survey of Jewish Education in Los Angeles* (Los Angeles: Jewish Community Council, 1944), 25.

261. Wertheimer, "Jewish Education in the United States," 18.

262. Idem, "Recent Trends in American Judaism," 115.

263. Mordecai Gifter, "The Function of Torah *Chinuch* in Our Generation," in *Hebrew Day School Education,* ed. Joseph Kaminetsky (New York: Torah Umesorah, National Society for Hebrew Day Schools, 1970), 18.

264. Ibid., 21.

265. On the development of Satmar's Kiryas Joel as well as similar initiatives by other Hasidic communities transplanted to the U.S., see Jerome R. Mintz, *Hasidic People: A Place in the New World* (Cambridge, Mass.: Harvard University Press, 1992).

266. Joseph Lookstein, "The Jewish Day School," in *Jewish Schools in America* (New York: American Association for Jewish Education, 1946), 32.

267. Wertheimer, "Recent Trends in American Judaism," 66.

268. Emanuel Gamoran, "Liberal Judaism and the Day School," *The Jewish Teacher* 19, no. 2 (January 1951): 6.

269. Pamela S. Nadell, *Conservative Judaism in America: A Biographical Dictionary and Sourcebook* (New York: Greenwood, 1988), 345.

270. United Synagogue Commission on Jewish Education, "Objectives and Standards for the Congregational School" (New York: United Synagogue, 1958), 22.

271. Wertheimer, "Jewish Education in the United States," 21.

272. A Gallup poll in 1979 with the question: Do "children today get a better—or worse—education than you did?" found that a minority, 41 percent, felt that their children's public education was superior to their own. Tyack and Cuban, *Tinkering toward Utopia*, 30.

273. Samuel Heilman, *Sliding to the Right* (Berkeley: University of California Press, 2006), 47.

274. American Jewish Archives, Small Collections–11037.

275. Quoted in Michael Zeldin, "A Century Later and Worlds Apart: American Jews and the Public School–Private School Dilemma, 1870, 1970," American Jewish Archives, Small Collections–13885 (Los Angeles, 1986), 40.

276. Michael Zeldin, "What Makes a Reform Day School Reform?" Paper delivered to first Reform day school conference, January 18, 1987. American Jewish Archives Small Collections–11031.

277. Zeldin, "A Century Later and Worlds Apart," 35–36.

278. Tyack and Cuban, *Tinkering toward Utopia*, 66–67.

279. Alexander Dushkin and Uriah Engleman, eds., *Jewish Education in the United States: Report of the Commission for the Study of Jewish Education in the United States* (New York: American Association for Jewish Education, 1959), 44.

280. Ibid., 114–16.

281. Ibid., 238.

282. Walter Ackerman, "Jewish Education—For What?" *American Jewish Year Book* 70 (1969): 8. Decades earlier, in the late 1940s, Rabbi Albert Lewis of (Reform) Temple Isaiah in Los Angeles had commented: "There is not a single religious school here in Los Angeles with a faculty of teachers worthy to be found teaching in a religious institution. They are *amha-artzim* [ignoramuses] in the truest meaning of that term. . . . As it stands now, we would be better off to close most of our schools and let the children stay home than spend any time at all with these teachers." Quoted in Deborah Dash Moore, *To the Golden Cities* (New York: Free Press, 1994), 135.

283. Ackerman, "Jewish Education—For What?" 8.

284. Kaufman, "Jewish Education as a Civilization," 617–18.

285. See Aron, "From the Congregational School to the Learning Congregation," 65.

286. Barnett Brickner, "President's Message," *CCAR Yearbook* 65 (1955): 15.

287. Walter I. Ackerman, "Toward a History of the Curriculum of the Conservative Congregational School," *Jewish Education* 48, no. 1 (1980): 21.

288. Krasner, "Representations of Self and Other," 432.

289. Herbert W. Bomzer, *The Kolel in America* (New York: Shengold, 1985), 19.

290. Ibid., 19.

291. Helmreich, *The World of the Yeshiva*, 257.

292. Sarna, *American Judaism*, 346.

293. Walter I. Ackerman, "Becoming Ramah," in *Forward from 50*, ed. Sheldon Dorph (New York: National Ramah Commission, 1999), 8.

294. On the history and impact of Camp Achvah, see Gannes and Soshuk, "The Kvutzah and Camp Achvah," 61–69.

295. Ackerman, "Becoming Ramah," 10.

296. Sarna, "The Crucial Decade in Jewish Camping," 37–38.

297. Ackerman, "Becoming Ramah," 10.

298. Michael Brown, "It's Off to Camp We Go," in *Tradition Renewed*, ed. Wertheimer, 1:827.

299. Shuly Rubin Schwartz, "Ramah Philosophy and the Newman Revolution," *Jewish Education and Judaica in Honor of Louis Newman*, ed. Alexander M. Shapiro and Burton I. Cohen (New York: Ktav, 1984), 8.

300. Sarna, "The Crucial Decade in Jewish Camping," 41.

301. Brown, "It's Off to Camp We Go," 833. Louis Newman, who was later to head the Melton Center for Research in Jewish Education at the Seminary's Teachers Institute, directed the Wisconsin camp, 1951–53, and influenced the future direction of Ramah camping through his blend of progressive education with Ramah's core goals. See Schwartz, "Ramah Philosophy and the Newman Revolution," and Burton I. Cohen, "Louis Newman's Wisconsin Innovations and Their Effect on the Ramah Camping Movement," in *Studies in Jewish Education and Judaica in Honor of Louis Newman*, ed. Shapiro and Cohen.

302. Sarna, "The Crucial Decade in Jewish Camping," 44.

303. Ibid., 44.

304. Ibid., 28.

305. By the 1980s, it was estimated that 85,000 children had spent a portion of the summer at a Jewish residential summer camp in North America. Background materials for Commission on Jewish Education in North America, June 12, 1990.

306. "Proceedings of First NFTY Convention (1939)," 22. American Jewish Archives MSS Collection No. 266, Box 1, File 1.

307. In the decades prior to USY (starting in 1921), the United Synagogue had supported the Young People's League (YPL), groups of young men and women

over the age of eighteen. Some YPL groups were affiliated with United Synagogue congregations; others were independent. Nadell, *Conservative Judaism
in America,* 331.

308. The first twentieth-century Jewish center to be established by the immigrant
community for its own use was the Chicago Hebrew Institute (1903). David
Kaufman, *Shul with a Pool: The Synagogue Center in American Jewish History* (Hanover, N.H.: University Press of New England, 1999), 118.
309. Marshall Sklare, *America's Jews* (New York: Random House, 1971), 139.
310. Oscar I. Janowsky, *The Jewish Community Center: Two Essays on Basic Purpose* (New York: National Jewish Welfare Board, 1974), 12.
311. Jack Wertheimer, "Jewish Organizational Life in the United States since 1945,"
American Jewish Year Book 95 (1995): 19.
312. On the origins of the JWB, see Kaufman, *Shul with a Pool,* 127. The study was
published as: Oscar I. Janowsky, *JWB Survey* (New York: Dial, 1948).
313. Janowsky, *The Jewish Community Center,* 13.
314. Egon Mayer, *From Suburb to Shtetl: The Jews of Boro Park* (Philadelphia:
Temple University Press, 1979), 38.
315. Arnold Band, "Jewish Studies in American Liberal Arts Colleges and Universities," in *The Education of American Jewish Teachers,* ed. Oscar I. Janowsky
(Boston: Beacon, 1967), 263.
316. On adult Jewish education until the middle of the twentieth century, see Harry
Elkin, "Adult Jewish Education Developments in the United States During the
Nineteenth and Twentieth Centuries," *Jewish Education* 26, no. 1 (summer
1955): 40–54.
317. Oscar I. Janowsky, "Adult Jewish Education: Analysis of a Survey," *Jewish Education* 36, no. 1 (fall 1965): 20. See also Samuel I. Cohen, "New Directions
in Adult Jewish Education," *Jewish Education* 38, no. 2 (March 1968): 5–14.
318. Wertheimer, "Recent Trends in American Judaism," 150.
319. Ibid., 153.
320. See Sylvia Barack Fishman, "The Impact of Feminism on American Jewish
Life," *American Jewish Year Book* 89 (1989): 3–62.
321. Karp, *A History of the Jews in America,* 308.
322. Wertheimer, "Jewish Organizational Life," 34.
323. Liebman, *The Ambivalent American Jew,* vii.
324. Barry Chazan, "Education in the Synagogue: The Transformation of the Supplementary School," in *The American Synagogue,* ed. Wertheimer, 181.
325. Himmelfarb, "The Impact of Religious Schooling"; and Bock, "The Jewish
Schooling of American Jews."
326. Harold S. Himmelfarb, "Jewish Education for Naught: Educating the Culturally Deprived Jewish Child," *Analysis,* Institute for Jewish Policy Planning
and Research of the Synagogue Council of America, no. 51 (Washington,
D.C., September 1975), 16. The Bock and Himmelfarb studies were criticized

methodologically in later years, but their findings stirred considerable discussion at the time.

327. Charles Zibbell, "Federations, Synagogues and Jewish Education in the 70s," *Jewish Education* 43, no. 3 (fall 1974): 41.

328. Ackerman, "The Americanization of Jewish Education," 433–34.

329. Marvin Schick, ed., *A Census of Jewish Day Schools in the United States* (New York: Avi Chai Foundation, 2000).

330. Wertheimer, "Jewish Education in the United States." Another excellent look at Jewish continuity trends in the 1990s is offered in Jonathan Woocher, "Toward a 'Unified Field Theory' of Jewish Continuity" (New York: Jewish Education Service of North America, 1994).

331. See United Jewish Communities, National Jewish Population Survey 2000–2001, 16–17, for discussion of the methodological basis for the disparity between the 52 percent and 43 percent figures.

332. Commission on Jewish Education in North America, *A Time to Act* (Lanham, Md.: University Press of America, 1990), 25–27.

333. Janice Prager and Arlene Lepoff, *Why Be Different?* (West Orange, N.J.: Behrman House, 1986).

334. David Wolpe, *Why Be Jewish?* (New York: H. Holt, 1995).

335. Wertheimer, "Jewish Education in the United States," 48.

336. See, for example, Marshall J. Breger and David M. Gordis, eds., *Vouchers for School Choice: Challenge or Opportunity?* (Boston: Wilstein Institute of Jewish Policy Studies, 1998).

337. By the beginning of the twenty-first century, elementary day school tuitions exceeding $10,000 and high school tuitions approaching $20,000 posed a considerable barrier to many who might have sought access. The challenges of meeting operational needs left few schools with the capacity to make day school education available to those with significant special learning needs. For most such students, not even the capacity to pay full tuition could make day school inclusion accessible.

338. Chazan, "Education in the Synagogue," 180.

339. See Michael Zeldin, "Integration and Interaction in the Jewish Day School," in *The Jewish Educational Leader's Handbook,* ed. Robert E. Tornberg (Denver: A.R.E., 1998), 579–90.

340. "Jewish Supplementary Schooling: An Educational System in Need of Change," a report by the Board of Jewish Education of Greater New York (New York: Board of Jewish Education, 1987).

341. See Adrianne Bank and Ron Wolfson, eds., *First Fruit: A Whizin Anthology of Jewish Family Education* (Los Angeles: Shirley and Arthur Whizin Institute for Jewish Family Life, 1998).

342. Joseph Reimer, *Succeeding at Jewish Education: How One Synagogue Made It Work* (Philadelphia: Jewish Publication Society, 1997).

343. Isa Aron, *Becoming a Congregation of Learners* (Woodstock, Vt.: Jewish Lights, 2000), 28.
344. Michael A. Meyer, "Reflections on the Educated Jew from the Perspective of Reform Judaism," in *Visions of Jewish Education,* ed. Seymour Fox, Israel Scheffler, and Daniel Marom (Cambridge: Cambridge University Press, 2003), 152.
345. Ibid., 160–61.
346. Gold, *Making the Bible Modern,* 199.
347. Moshe Greenberg, "We Were as Those Who Dream: An Agenda for an Ideal Jewish Education," in *Visions of Jewish Education,* ed. Fox et al., 123.
348. On the growing disparity between "resistance" and "accommodation" in Orthodox Jewish life and its impact on education, see Heilman, *Sliding to the Right,* 78–126.
349. Steven M. Cohen and Arnold Eisen, *The Jew Within* (Bloomington: Indiana University Press, 2000), 205.
350. CCAR Statement of Principles, adopted May 26, 1999.
351. Ismar Schorsch, "The Sacred Cluster" (Jewish Theological Seminary, 1995), 2.
352. Ibid., 3.
353. Sarna, *American Judaism,* 329.
354. Bernard D. Cooperman, "Jewish Studies in the University," in *Jewish Identity in America,* ed. David M. Gordis and Yoav Ben-Horin (Los Angeles: Wilstein Institute, 1991), 199.
355. Helmreich, *The World of the Yeshiva,* xviii.
356. Ibid.
357. Sarna, *American Judaism,* 363–64. The declining sense of Jewish peoplehood among American Jews is well described in Steven M. Cohen and Jack Wertheimer, "Whatever Happened to the Jewish People?" *Commentary* 121, no. 6 (June 2006): 33–37.
358. The Reconstructionist movement adopted this stance in 1968. Inasmuch as the Reconstructionists were a new entry in the denominational streams of American Jewish life and had little market share, it was the decision of the Reform movement that elicited attention and reaction.
359. See Emil Jacoby, *Accreditation Manual for Jewish Schools* (Los Angeles: Bureau of Jewish Education, 1998).
360. Dushkin, *Jewish Education in New York City,* 394.
361. United Jewish Communities, National Jewish Population Survey 2000–2001, 2–3.
362. Ibid., 4.
363. Ibid., 10.
364. Ibid., 16–17.
365. Ibid., 15.
366. Ibid.

367. Steven M. Cohen, "Jewish Identity Research in the United States: Ruminations on Concepts and Findings" (Hebrew University, 2002), 24.

368. Salo W. Baron, "The Modern Age," in *Great Ages and Ideas of the Jewish People*, ed. Leo W. Schwarz (New York: Random House, 1956), 483–84.

369. Simon Rawidowicz, "Israel: The Ever-Dying People," in *Israel: The Ever-Dying People and Other Essays*, ed. Benjamin C. I. Ravid (Rutherford, N.J.: Fairleigh Dickinson University Press, 1986), 54.

370. Tyack and Cuban, *Tinkering toward Utopia*, 3.

371. Marvin Schick, *A Census of Jewish Day Schools in the United States* (New York: Avi Chai Foundation, 2005).

372. Commission on Jewish Education in North America, *A Time to Act*, 19.

Bibliography

Ackerman, Walter I. "The Americanization of Jewish Education." *Judaism* 24, no. 4 (fall 1975): 416–35.

___. "Becoming Ramah." In *Forward from 50*, ed. Sheldon Dorph, 3–24. New York: National Ramah Commission, 1999.

___. "Jewish Education—For What?" *American Jewish Year Book* 70 (1969): 3–36.

___. "New Models of Jewish Education: Formal and Informal—What Learning Is Most Worth." *Jewish Education* 54, no. 2 (summer 1986): 3–7.

___. "Toward a History of the Curriculum of the Conservative Congregational School." *Jewish Education* 48, no. 1 (spring 1980): 19–26.

___. "What We Know About Schools." In *What We Know About Jewish Education*, ed. Stuart L. Kelman, 21–32. Los Angeles: Torah Aura, 1992.

American Jewish Archives. "Petition (1961) Calling Upon Commission on Jewish Education to Investigate Establishment of Day Schools." Small Collections–11037.

___. "Proceedings of the First NFTY Convention (1939)." MSS Collection No. 266, Box 1, File 1.

Angel, Marc D. "The Sephardim of the United States: An Exploratory Study." *American Jewish Year Book* 74 (1973): 77–138.

Aron, Isa. *Becoming a Congregation of Learners.* Woodstock, Vt.: Jewish Lights, 2000.

___. "From the Congregational School to the Learning Congregation." In *A Congregation of Learners*, ed. Isa Aron, Sara Lee, and Seymour Rossel, 56–77. New York: Union of American Hebrew Congregations Press, 1995.

Ashton, Dianne. *Rebecca Gratz: Women and Judaism in Antebellum America.* Detroit: Wayne State University Press, 1997.

Band, Arnold. "Jewish Studies in American Liberal Arts Colleges and Universities." In *The Education of American Jewish Teachers*, ed. Oscar I. Janowsky, 255–64. Boston: Beacon, 1967.

Bank, Adrianne, and Ron Wolfson, eds. *First Fruit: A Whizin Anthology of Jewish*

Family Education. Los Angeles: Shirley and Arthur Whizin Institute for Jewish Family Life, 1998.

Barkai, Avraham. *Branching Out: German-Jewish Immigration to the United States, 1820–1914.* New York: Holmes and Meier, 1994.

Baron, Salo W. "The Modern Age." In *Great Ages and Ideas of the Jewish People,* ed. Leo W. Schwarz, 315–484. New York: Random House, 1956.

Benderly, Samson. "Jewish Education in America." *Jewish Education* 20, no. 3 (summer 1949): 80–86. Reprint.

___. "Letter of Samson Benderly to Judah Magnes, March 9, 1910." *Jewish Education* 20, no. 3 (summer 1949): 110–12. Reprint.

Ben-Horin, Meir. "From the Turn of the Century to the Late Thirties." In *A History of Jewish Education in America,* ed. Judah Pilch, 51–118. New York: American Association for Jewish Education, 1969.

Ben-Sasson, H. H., ed. *A History of the Jewish People.* Cambridge, Mass.: Harvard University Press, 1976.

Berkowitz, Max. *The Beloved Rabbi: An Account of the Life and Works of Henry Berkowitz.* New York: Macmillan, 1932.

Berkson, Isaac B., and Ben Rosen. "Jewish Education Survey of Cleveland." *Jewish Education* 9, no. 1 (January–March 1937): 12–19.

Berman, Myron. *Richmond's Jewry.* Charlottesville: University of Virginia Press, 1979.

Blau, Joseph L., and Salo W. Baron, eds. *The Jews of the United States 1790–1840: A Documentary History.* 3 vols. New York: Columbia University Press, 1963.

Board of Jewish Education of Greater New York. "Jewish Supplementary Schooling: An Educational System in Need of Change." New York: Board of Jewish Education, 1987.

Bock, Geoffrey F. "The Jewish Schooling of American Jews: A Study of Non-Cognitive Educational Effects." Ph.D. diss., Harvard University, 1976.

Bomzer, Herbert W. *The Kolel in America.* New York: Shengold, 1985.

Boyer, Paul S., Clifford E. Clark, Jr., Joseph F. Kett, Neal Salisbury, and Harvard Sitkoff. *The Enduring Vision: A History of the American People.* Vol. 1. Lexington, Mass.: D. C. Heath, 1996.

Breger, Marshall J., and David M. Gordis, eds. *Vouchers for School Choice: Challenge or Opportunity?* Boston: Wilstein Institute of Jewish Policy Studies, 1998.

Brickner, Barnett. "President's Message." *CCAR Yearbook* 65 (1955): 3–18.

Brown, Michael. "It's Off to Camp We Go." In *Tradition Renewed: A History of the Jewish Theological Seminary of America,* ed. Jack Wertheimer, 1:823–54. New York: Jewish Theological Seminary, 1997.

Central Conference of American Rabbis (CCAR). "Statement of Principles for Reform Judaism." Pittsburgh: CCAR, 1999.

Chazan, Barry. "Education in the Synagogue: The Transformation of the Supplementary School." In *The American Synagogue: A Sanctuary Transformed,* ed. Jack Wertheimer, 170–84. New York: Cambridge University Press, 1987.

Citron, Samuel J. "Dr. Benderly's Love of Drama." *Jewish Education* 20, no. 3 (summer 1949): 70–74.

Cohen, Burton I. "Louis Newman's Wisconsin Innovations and Their Effect on the Ramah Camping Movement." In *Studies in Jewish Education and Judaica in Honor of Louis Newman,* ed. Alexander M. Shapiro and Burton I. Cohen, 23–38. New York: Ktav, 1984.

Cohen, Naomi W. *Encounter with Emancipation: The German Jews in the United States 1830–1914.* Philadelphia: Jewish Publication Society, 1984.

Cohen, Samuel I. "New Directions in Adult Jewish Education." *Jewish Education* 38, no. 2 (March 1968): 5–14.

Cohen, Steven M. "Jewish Identity Research in the United States: Ruminations on Concepts and Findings." Hebrew University, 2002.

Cohen, Steven M., and Arnold Eisen. *The Jew Within.* Bloomington: Indiana University Press, 2000.

Cohen, Steven M., and Jack Wertheimer. "Whatever Happened to the Jewish People?" *Commentary* 121, no. 6 (June 2006): 33–37.

Commission on Jewish Education in North America. Background materials, June 12, 1990.

___. *A Time to Act.* Lanham, Md.: University Press of America, 1990.

Cooperman, Bernard. "Jewish Studies in the University." In *Jewish Identity in America,* ed. David M. Gordis and Yoav Ben-Horin, 195–206. Los Angeles: Wilstein Institute, 1991.

Cremin, Lawrence A. *American Education: The National Experience, 1783–1876.* New York: Harper and Row, 1980.

___. *Traditions of American Education.* New York: Basic Books, 1977.

Davis, Moshe. *The Emergence of Conservative Judaism.* Philadelphia: Jewish Publication Society, 1963.

Diner, Hasia R. "Like the Antelope and the Badger." In *Tradition Renewed: A History of the Jewish Theological Seminary of America,* ed. Jack Wertheimer, 1:3–42. New York: Jewish Theological Seminary, 1997.

___. *The Jews of the United States, 1654–2000.* Berkeley: University of California Press, 2004.

Diner, Hasia R., and Beryl Lieff Benderly. *Her Works Praise Her: A History of Jewish Women in America from Colonial Times to the Present.* New York: Basic Books, 2002.

Dorff, Elliot. *Conservative Judaism: Our Ancestors to Our Descendants.* New York: United Synagogue of America Youth Commission, 1977.

Dorph, Sheldon A. "A New Direction for Jewish Education in America." In *Studies in Jewish Education and Judaica in Honor of Louis Newman,* ed. Alexander M. Shapiro and Burton I. Cohen, 99–115. New York: Ktav, 1984.

Drachler, Norman. *A Bibliography of Jewish Education in the United States.* Detroit: Wayne State University Press, 1996.

Drachman, Bernard. *The Unfailing Light*. New York: Rabbinical Council of America, 1948.

Dushkin, Alexander. *Jewish Education in New York City*. New York: Bureau of Jewish Education, 1918.

———. *Survey of Jewish Education in Los Angeles*. Los Angeles: Jewish Community Council, 1944.

Dushkin, Alexander, and Uriah Engleman, eds. *Jewish Education in the United States: Report of the Commission for the Study of Jewish Education in the United States*. New York: American Association for Jewish Education, 1959.

Ehrlich, Walter. *Zion in the Valley: The Jewish Community of St. Louis*. Columbia: University of Missouri Press, 2002.

Einhorn, David. "Inaugural Sermon," trans. C. A. Rubenstein. Baltimore, 1909.

Elkin, Harry. "Adult Jewish Education Developments in the United States During the Nineteenth and Twentieth Centuries." *Jewish Education* 26 (summer 1955): 40–54.

Ellenson, David. *Tradition in Transition*. Lanham, Md.: University Press of America, 1989.

Ellenson, David, and Lee Bycel. "A Seminary of Sacred Learning." In *Tradition Renewed: A History of the Jewish Theological Seminary of America*, ed. Jack Wertheimer, 2:526–91. New York: Jewish Theological Seminary, 1997.

Faber, Eli. "The Formative Era of American Jewish History." *American Jewish History* 86, no. 1 (autumn 1993): 9–21.

Farber, Seth. *An American Orthodox Dreamer*. Hanover, N.H.: University Press of New England, 2004.

Feingold, Henry L. *A Time for Searching: Entering the Mainstream, 1920–1945*. Baltimore: Johns Hopkins University Press, 1992.

Felsenthal, Emma, ed. *Bernard Felsenthal: Teacher in Israel*. New York: Oxford University Press, 1924.

Feuer, Lewis S. "The Golden Age of the Downtown Talmud Torah in New York's Lower East Side." Unpublished memoir. American Jewish Archives Small Collections–13784.

Fierman, Floyd S. *Sources of Jewish Education in America Prior to 1881*. El Paso, Tex., 1960.

Fishman, Sylvia Barack. "The Impact of Feminism on American Jewish Life." *American Jewish Year Book* 89 (1989): 3–62.

———. *Jewish Life and American Culture*. Albany, N.Y.: State University of New York Press, 2000.

Gamoran, Emanuel. "The Jewish Sunday School." In *Jewish Schools in America*, 44–49. New York: American Association for Jewish Education, 1946.

———. "Liberal Judaism and the Day School." *The Jewish Teacher* 19, no. 2 (January 1951): 1–6.

———. "Recent Tendencies in Education and Their Application to the Jewish School." *CCAR Yearbook* 33 (1923): 314–27.

Gamoran, Mamie. *Hillel's Happy Holidays.* Cincinnati: Union of American Hebrew Congregations, 1939.

Gannes, Abraham P. *Central Community Agencies for Jewish Education.* Philadelphia: Dropsie College, 1954.

___, ed. *Selected Writings of Leo L. Honor.* New York: Reconstructionist Press, 1965.

Gannes, Abraham P., and Levi Soshuk. "The Kvutzah and Camp Achvah." *Jewish Education* 20, no. 3 (summer 1949): 61–69.

Gartner, Lloyd P. "Immigration and the Formation of American Jewry, 1840–1925." In *Jewish Society Through the Ages,* ed. H. H. Ben-Sasson and S. Ettinger, 297–312. London: Vallentine, Mitchell, 1971.

___, ed. *Jewish Education in the United States: A Documentary History.* New York: Teachers College Press, 1969.

___. "Jewish Migrants En Route from Europe to North America: Traditions and Realities." *Jewish History* 1, no. 2 (fall 1986): 49–66.

___. "Temples of Liberty Unpolluted: American Jews and Public Schools." In *A Bicentennial Festschrift for Jacob Rader Marcus,* ed. Bertram W. Korn, 157–89. New York: Ktav, 1976.

Gifter, Mordecai. "The Function of Torah *Chinuch* in Our Generation." In *Hebrew Day School Education,* ed. Joseph Kaminetsky, 18–24. New York: Torah Umesorah, National Society for Hebrew Day Schools, 1970.

Ginsburgh, Stanley A. "A Study of Nationally Organized Jewish Youth Groups in America as Agencies for the Preservation of the Jewish Cultural Heritage." Diss., Massachusetts State College, 1940. American Jewish Archives, Microfilm #74.

Gold, Penny Schine. *Making the Bible Modern.* Ithaca, N.Y.: Cornell University Press, 2004.

Goren, Arthur A. *Jews and the Quest for Community: The Kehilla Experiment.* New York: Columbia University Press, 1970.

___. "Spiritual Zionists and Jewish Sovereignty." In *The Americanization of the Jews,* ed. Robert M. Seltzer and Norman J. Cohen, 165–92. New York: New York University Press, 1995.

Graff, Gil. "Jewish Education in the United States of America." *Encyclopaedia Judaica.* 2nd ed. (2007), 6:189–204.

___. "Public Schooling and Jewish Education, 1845–1870: A Contemporary Perspective." *Journal of Jewish Education* 69, no. 1 (spring–summer 2003): 69–76.

Greenberg, Moshe. "We Were as Those Who Dream: An Agenda for an Ideal Jewish Education." In *Visions of Jewish Education,* ed. Seymour Fox, Israel Scheffler, and Daniel Marom, 122–32. Cambridge: Cambridge University Press, 2003.

Greenberg, Simon. "The Congregational School Three Days a Week." In *Jewish Schools in America,* 13–19. New York: American Association for Jewish Education, 1946.

Greenstone, Julius. "Jewish Education in the United States." *American Jewish Year Book* 16 (1914–15): 90–127.

Grinstein, Hyman. "In the Course of the Nineteenth Century." In *A History of Jewish Education in America,* ed. Judah Pilch, 25–50. New York: American Association for Jewish Education, 1969.

___. *The Rise of the Jewish Community of New York, 1654–1860.* Philadelphia: Jewish Publication Society, 1947.

Gurock, Jeffrey S. "The Ramaz Version of American Orthodoxy." In *RAMAZ: School, Community, Scholarship and Orthodoxy,* ed. idem, 40–82. Hoboken, N.J.: Ktav, 1989.

___. "Resisters and Accommodators: Varieties of Orthodox Rabbis in America, 1886–1983." In *American Jewish Orthodoxy in Historical Perspective,* ed. idem, 1–62. Hoboken, N.J.: Ktav, 1996.

Gutek, Gerald L. *A History of the Western Educational Experience.* Prospect Heights, Ill.: Waveland, 1995.

Hagy, James W. *This Happy Land: The Jews of Colonial and Antebellum Charleston.* Tuscaloosa: University of Alabama Press, 1993.

Hartstein, Jacob. "The Polonies Talmud Torah of New York." *Publications of the American Jewish Historical Society* 34 (1937): 123–41.

Heilman, Samuel. *Portrait of American Jews.* Seattle: University of Washington Press, 1995.

___. *Sliding to the Right: The Contest for the Future of American Jewish Orthodoxy.* Berkeley: University of California Press, 2006.

Heller, James G. *Isaac M. Wise.* New York: Union of American Hebrew Congregations, 1965.

Helmreich, William B. *The World of the Yeshiva: An Intimate Portrait of Orthodox Jewry.* Augmented ed. Hoboken, N.J.: Ktav, 2000.

Hertzberg, Arthur. *The Jews in America: Four Centuries of an Uneasy Encounter.* New York: Simon and Schuster, 1989.

___. "Seventy Years of Jewish Education." *Judaism* 1, no. 4 (October 1952): 361–65.

___, ed. *The Zionist Idea.* Philadelphia: Jewish Publication Society, 1997.

Himmelfarb, Harold S. *Analysis No. 51,* Institute for Jewish Policy Planning and Research of the Synagogue Council of America. Washington, D.C., 1975.

___. "The Impact of Religious Schooling: The Effects of Jewish Education upon Adult Religious Involvement." Ph.D. diss., University of Chicago, 1975.

Illoway, Henry. *Sefer Milkhamot Elohim: The Controversial Letters and the Casuistic Decisions of the Late Rabbi Bernard Illowy, Ph.D.* Berlin: M. Poppelauer, 1914.

Jacoby, Emil. *Accreditation Manual for Jewish Schools.* Los Angeles: Bureau of Jewish Education, 1998.

Janowsky, Oscar I. "Adult Jewish Education: Analysis of a Survey." *Jewish Education* 36, no. 1 (fall 1965): 17–23.

___. *The American Jew: A Reappraisal.* Philadelphia: Jewish Publication Society, 1964.

___, ed. *The Education of American Jewish Teachers.* Boston: Beacon, 1967.

___. *The Jewish Community Center: Two Essays on Basic Purpose.* New York: National Jewish Welfare Board, 1974.

___. *JWB Survey.* New York: Dial, 1948.

Jick, Leon. *The Americanization of the Synagogue, 1820–1870.* Hanover, N.H.: Brandeis University Press, 1992.

J. K. G. (of Boston). "Objects and Means of Religious Education." *The Occident* 2 (1844): 185–95.

Joselit, Jenna Weissman. *New York's Jewish Jews: The Orthodox Community in the Interwar Years.* Bloomington: Indiana University Press, 1990.

___. *The Wonders of America: Reinventing Jewish Culture, 1880–1950.* New York: Hill and Wang, 1994.

Jung, Leo, and Joseph Kaminetsky, eds. *A Model Program for the Talmud Torah.* New York: Union of Orthodox Jewish Congregations of America, 1942.

Kabakoff, Jacob. "The Use of Hebrew by American Jews During the Colonial Period." In *Hebrew and the Bible in America: The First Two Centuries,* ed. Shalom Goldman, 191–98. Hanover, N.H.: University Press of New England, 1993.

Kaplan, Mordecai M. *Judaism as a Civilization: Toward a Reconstruction of American-Jewish Life.* Philadelphia: Jewish Publication Society, 1994. New ed.; 1ˢᵗ ed., 1934.

Karp, Abraham J. *A History of the Jews in America.* Northvale, N.J.: J. Aronson, 1997.

___. *Jewish Continuity in America.* Tuscaloosa: University of Alabama Press, 1998.

Kaufman, David. "Jewish Education as a Civilization." In *Tradition Renewed: A History of the Jewish Theological Seminary of America,* ed. Jack Wertheimer, 1:567–629. New York: Jewish Theological Seminary, 1997.

___. *Shul with a Pool: The Synagogue Center in American Jewish History.* Hanover, N.H.: University Press of New England, 1999.

Klapper, Melissa. "'A Fair Portion of the World's Knowledge': Jewish Girls Coming of Age in America, 1860–1920." Ph.D. diss., Rutgers University, 2001.

Klapperman, Gilbert. *The Story of Yeshiva University.* New York: Macmillan, 1969.

Kohler, Kaufmann. "A Biographical Essay." In *David Einhorn Memorial Volume,* ed. idem, 403–55. New York: Bloch, 1911.

Kramer, Doniel Z. *The Day Schools and Torah Umesorah.* New York: Yeshiva University Press, 1984.

Krasner, Jonathan B. "Representations of Self and Other in American Jewish History and Social Studies School Books: An Exploration of the Changing Shape of American Jewish Identity." Ph.D. diss., Brandeis University, 2002.

Lapson, Dvora. "An Intuitive Approach to the Dance." *Jewish Education* 20, no. 3 (summer 1949): 75–76.

Leeser, Isaac. *Catechism for Younger Children: Designed as a Religious Manual for House and School.* Philadelphia: Sherman, 1839.

___. *Discourses* III. Philadelphia, 1841.

___. *Discourses* X. Philadelphia, 1867.

___. *The Hebrew Reader: Designed as an Easy Guide to the Hebrew Tongue, for Jewish Children and Self-Instruction.* Philadelphia: Sherman, 1838; 4th ed., 1856.

___. "Jewish Children under Gentile Teachers." *The Occident* 1 (1843): 409–14.

___. "A Plea for Education." *The Occident* 4 (1846): 109–14.

___. "'The Testimony': An Address Delivered Nisan 5611." Philadelphia, 1851.

Levinger, Lee. *A History of the Jews in the United States.* Cincinnati: Union of American Hebrew Congregations, 1930.

Liebman, Charles. *The Ambivalent American Jew.* Philadelphia: Jewish Publication Society, 1973.

___. "American Jewry: Identity and Affiliation." In *The Future of the Jewish Community in America,* ed. David Sidorsky, 127–54. Philadelphia: Jewish Publication Society, 1973.

Lookstein, Joseph. "The Jewish Day School." In *Jewish Schools in America,* 28–35. New York: American Association for Jewish Education, 1946.

Lorge, Michael M., and Gary P. Zola, eds. *A Place of Our Own: The Rise of Reform Jewish Camping.* Tuscaloosa: University of Alabama Press, 2006.

Lyons Collection, Archives of the American Jewish Historical Society.

Marcus, Jacob R. "The American Colonial Jew: A Study in Acculturation." In *The American Jewish Experience,* ed. Jonathan D. Sarna, 6–19. New York: Holmes and Meier, 1997.

___. *The American Jew: 1585–1990.* Brooklyn, N.Y.: Carlson, 1995.

___, ed. *The American Jewish Woman: A Documentary History.* New York: Ktav, 1981.

___. *The Handsome Young Priest in the Black Gown.* Cincinnati: American Jewish Archives, 1970.

___. *The Jew in the American World.* Detroit: Wayne State University Press, 1996.

___. *United States Jewry, 1776–1985.* Detroit: Wayne State University Press, 1989.

Margolis, Isidor. *Jewish Teacher Training Schools in the United States.* New York: National Council for Torah Education of Mizrachi–Hapoel Hamizrachi, 1964.

Mayer, Egon. *From Suburb to Shtetl: The Jews of Boro Park.* Philadelphia: Temple University Press, 1979.

Mendes-Flohr, Paul R., and Jehuda Reinharz, eds. *The Jew in the Modern World.* New York: Oxford University Press, 1995.

Merowitz, Morton J. "Max Lilienthal (1814–1882): Jewish Educator in Nineteenth-Century America." *YIVO Annual of Jewish Social Science* 15 (1974): 46–65.

Meyer, Michael A. "America: The Reform Movement's Land of Promise." In *The American Jewish Experience,* ed. Jonathan D. Sarna, 60–83. New York: Holmes and Meier, 1997.

___. *Judaism within Modernity.* Detroit: Wayne State University Press, 2001.

___. "Reflections on the Educated Jew from the Perspective of Reform Judaism." In

Visions of Jewish Education, ed. Seymour Fox, Israel Scheffler, and Daniel Marom, 149–61. Cambridge: Cambridge University Press, 2003.

___. *Response to Modernity.* Detroit: Wayne State University Press, 1995.

Meyer, Michael A., and W. Gunther Plaut, eds. *The Reform Judaism Reader.* New York: Union of American Hebrew Congregations Press, 2001.

Mielziner, Moses. "Pedagogics in the Sabbath School." In *Moses Mielziner,* ed. Ella McKenna Friend Mielziner, 116–26. New York, 1931.

Mintz, Alan, ed. *Hebrew in America.* Detroit: Wayne State University Press, 1993.

Mintz, Jerome R. *Hasidic People: A Place in the New World.* Cambridge, Mass.: Harvard University Press, 1992.

Moore, Deborah Dash. *To the Golden Cities.* New York: Free Press, 1994.

Nadell, Pamela S. *Conservative Judaism in America: A Biographical Dictionary and Sourcebook.* New York: Greenwood, 1988.

Nathanson, Moshe. "Dr. Benderly as Impresario." *Jewish Education* 20, no. 3 (summer 1949): 77–78.

Pearlstein, Peggy Kronsberg. "Understanding through Education: One Hundred Years of the Jewish Chautauqua Society," 1893–1993. Ph.D. diss., George Washington University, 1993.

Petuchowski, Jacob J. "Manuals and Catechisms of the Jewish Religion in the Early Period of Emancipation." In *Studies in Nineteenth-Century Jewish Intellectual History,* ed. Alexander Altmann, 47–64. Cambridge, Mass.: Harvard University Press, 1964.

Pilch, Judah, ed. "From the Early Forties to the Mid-Sixties." In *A History of Jewish Education in America,* ed. idem, 119–76. New York: American Association for Jewish Education, 1969.

Pool, David deSola. "George Washington and Religious Liberty." New York, 1932.

Prager, Janice, and Arlene Lepoff. *Why Be Different?* West Orange, N.J.: Behrman House, 1986.

Rabinowitz, Benjamin. *The Young Men's Hebrew Associations, 1854–1913.* New York: National Jewish Welfare Board, 1948.

Rakeffet-Rothkoff, Aaron. "The Attempt to Merge the JTS and Yeshiva College, 1926–27." *Michael* 3 (1975): 254–80.

Raphael, Marc Lee. *Judaism in America.* New York: Columbia University Press, 2003.

___. *Profiles in American Judaism.* San Francisco: Harper and Row, 1984.

Rauch, Eduardo. *The Education of Jews and the American Community: 1840 to the New Millennium.* Tel Aviv: Tel Aviv University, 2004.

___. "Jewish Education in the United States: 1840–1920." Ed.D. diss., Harvard University, 1978.

Rawidowicz, Simon. "Israel: The Ever-Dying People." In *Israel: The Ever-Dying People and Other Essays,* ed. Benjamin C. I. Ravid, 53–63. Rutherford, N.J.: Fairleigh Dickinson University Press, 1986.

Reimer, Joseph. *Succeeding at Jewish Education: How One Synagogue Made It Work*. Philadelphia: Jewish Publication Society, 1997.

Reznikoff, Charles. *The Jews of Charleston*. Philadelphia: Jewish Publication Society, 1950.

Rothkoff, Aaron. *Bernard Revel: Builder of American Jewish Orthodoxy*. Philadelphia: Jewish Publication Society, 1972.

Rubin, Saul J. *Third to None: The Saga of Savannah Jewry*. Savannah, Ga.: Mickve Israel, 1983.

Ruderman, David B. *Jewish Enlightenment in an English Key*. Princeton, N.J.: Princeton University Press, 2000.

Sacks, Jonathan. *The Dignity of Difference*. London: Continuum, 2003.

Sarna, Jonathan D. "American Jewish Education in Historical Perspective." *Jewish Education* 64, nos. 1–2 (winter/spring 1998): 8–21.

___. *American Judaism*. New Haven, Conn.: Yale University Press, 2004.

___. "The Crucial Decade in Jewish Camping." In *A Place of Our Own: The Rise of Reform Jewish Camping*, ed. Michael M. Lorge and Gary P. Zola, 27–51. Tuscaloosa: University of Alabama Press, 2006.

___. "The Cyclical History of Adult Jewish Learning in the United States: Peers' Law and Its Implications." In *Educational Deliberations: Studies in Education Dedicated to Shlomo (Seymour) Fox*, ed. Mordecai Nisan and Oded Schremer, 207–22. Jerusalem: Keter, 2005.

___. "From Synagogue-Community to Community of Synagogues: A Turning Point in American History." Brandeis University, 1990.

___. *A Great Awakening: The Transformation That Shaped Twentieth-Century American Judaism and Its Implications for Today*. New York: Council for Initiatives in Jewish Education, 1995.

___. "The Jewish Experience in American Public and Private Education." In *Vouchers for School Choice: Challenge or Opportunity?*, ed. Marshall J. Breger and David M. Gordis, 131–36. Boston: Wilstein Institute of Jewish Policy Studies, 1998.

___. "Jewish Identity in the Changing World of American Religion." In *Jewish Identity in America*, ed. David M. Gordis and Yoav Ben-Horin, 91–103. Los Angeles: Wilstein Institute, 1991.

Sarna, Jonathan D., and David G. Dalin, eds. *Religion and State in the American Jewish Experience*. Notre Dame, Ind.: University of Notre Dame Press, 1997.

Scharfstein, Zevi. *Arbaim shana be-Amerikah*. Tel Aviv: Masadah, 1956.

___. *History of Jewish Education* [in Hebrew]. 5 vols. Jerusalem: R. Mas, 1960–65.

Schick, Marvin, ed. *A Census of Jewish Day Schools in the United States*. New York: Avi Chai Foundation, 2000.

___. *A Census of Jewish Day Schools in the United States*. New York: Avi Chai Foundation, 2005.

Schiff, Alvin. *The Jewish Day School in America*. New York: Jewish Education Committee Press, 1966.

___. *The Mystique of Hebrew: An Ancient Language in the New World.* New York: Shengold, 1996.

Schoem, David. *Ethnic Survival in America: An Ethnography of a Jewish Afternoon School.* Atlanta: Scholars Press, 1989.

Schoenfeld, Stuart. "Folk Judaism, Elite Judaism and the Role of the Bar Mitzvah in the Development of the Synagogue and Jewish School in America." *Contemporary Jewry* 9 (1988): 67–85.

Schorsch, Ismar. "The Sacred Cluster." Jewish Theological Seminary, 1995.

Schreiber, Emanuel. "How to Teach Biblical History in Our Sabbath Schools." *CCAR Proceedings* 1 (1890–91): 59–61.

Schwartz, Shuly Rubin. *The Emergence of Jewish Scholarship in America.* Cincinnati: Hebrew Union College Press, 1991.

___. "Ramah Philosophy and the Newman Revolution." In *Studies in Jewish Education and Judaica in Honor of Louis Newman,* ed. Alexander M. Shapiro and Burton I. Cohen, 7–21. New York: Ktav, 1984.

___. "Rebecca Aaronson Brickner: Preacher, Teacher, and Rebbetzin in Israel." *American Jewish Archives Journal* 54, no. 1 (2002): 65–83.

Scult, Mel, ed. *Communings of the Spirit: The Journals of Mordecai M. Kaplan, 1913–1934.* Detroit: Wayne State University Press, 2001.

___. *Judaism Faces the Twentieth Century: A Biography of Mordecai M. Kaplan.* Detroit: Wayne State University Press, 1993.

___. "Schechter's Seminary." In *Tradition Renewed: A History of the Jewish Theological Seminary of America,* ed. Jack Wertheimer, 1:45–102. New York: Jewish Theological Seminary, 1997.

Sharfman, I. Harold. *The First Rabbi.* Malibu, Calif.: Pangloss, 1988.

Silverstein, Alan. *Alternatives to Assimilation.* Hanover, N.H.: University Press of New England, 1994.

Sklare, Marshall. *America's Jews.* New York: Random House, 1971.

___. *Conservative Judaism: An American Religious Movement.* New York: Schocken, 1972.

Sorin, Gerald. *Tradition Transformed.* Baltimore: Johns Hopkins University Press, 1997.

Spicehandler, Ezra. "Hebrew Language and Literature at the Hebrew Union College–Jewish Institute of Religion, 1876–1930." In *Jewish Education and Learning,* ed. Glenda Abramson and Tudor Parfitt, 37–60. Langhome, Pa.: Harwood Academic Publishers, 1994.

Stampfer, Shaul. "Heder Study, Knowledge of Torah and the Maintenance of Social Stratification in Traditional East European Jewish Society." In *Studies in Jewish Education* 3 (1988): 271–89.

Stern, Miriam Heller. "A Dream Not Quite Come True: Reassessing the Benderly Era in Jewish Education." *Journal of Jewish Education* 70, no. 3 (fall 2004): 16–26.

Sussman, Lance J. *Isaac Leeser and the Making of American Judaism.* Detroit: Wayne State University Press, 1995.

___. "Jewish Intellectual Activity and Educational Practice in the United States: 1776–1840." American Jewish Archives Small Collections–12167. Cincinnati, 1978.

Swichkow, Louis J., and Lloyd P. Gartner. *History of the Jews of Milwaukee.* Philadelphia: Jewish Publication Society, 1963.

Temkin, Sefton D. *Isaac Mayer Wise.* Oxford: Oxford University Press, 1992.

Toll, William. "From Domestic Judaism to Public Ritual: Women and Religious Identity in the American West." In *Women and American Judaism,* ed. Pamela S. Nadell and Jonathan D. Sarna, 128–47. Hanover, N.H.: University Press of New England, 2001.

Tyack, David, and Larry Cuban. *Tinkering toward Utopia: A Century of Public School Reform.* Cambridge, Mass.: Harvard University Press, 1995.

United Jewish Communities. "National Jewish Population Survey 2000–01" (New York, 2003), http://www.ujc.org/page.html?ArticleID=33650.

United Synagogue Commission on Jewish Education. "Objectives and Standards for the Congregational School." New York: United Synagogue, 1958.

Vorspan, Max, and Lloyd P. Gartner. *History of the Jews in Los Angeles.* Philadelphia: Jewish Publication Society, 1970.

Weinberger, Moses. *People Walk on Their Heads,* trans. and ed. Jonathan D. Sarna. New York: Holmes and Meier, 1982.

Wertheimer, Jack. "The Conservative Synagogue." In *The American Synagogue: A Sanctuary Transformed,* ed. idem, 111–49. New York: Cambridge University Press, 1987.

___. "Jewish Education in the United States: Recent Trends and Issues." *American Jewish Yearbook* 99 (1999): 3–115.

___. "Jewish Organizational Life in the United States since 1945." *American Jewish Year Book* 95 (1995): 3–98.

___. "Recent Trends in American Judaism." *American Jewish Year Book* 89 (1989): 63–162.

___. *Talking Dollars and Sense about Jewish Education.* New York: Avi Chai Foundation, 2001.

___, ed. *Tradition Renewed: A History of the Jewish Theological Seminary of America.* 2 vols. New York: Jewish Theological Seminary, 1997.

Whitfield, Stephen J. "The Future of American Jewry: A History." *American Jewish Year Book* 104 (2004): 3–31.

Winter, Nathan H. *Jewish Education in a Pluralist Society.* New York: New York University Press, 1966.

Wise, Isaac Mayer. *The Essence of Judaism.* Cincinnati: Bloch, 1861.

___. *Judaism: Its Doctrines and Duties.* Cincinnati: Published in the office of *The Israelite,* 1872.

___. "The New American Jew: American Jewish Life as Seen from Albany, New York, September 1847," trans. Sefton D. Temkin. Albany, N.Y.: Congregation Beth Emeth, 1977.

Wolf, Edwin, and Maxwell Whiteman. *History of the Jews of Philadelphia.* Philadelphia: Jewish Publication Society, 1957.

Wolpe, David. *Why Be Jewish?* New York: H. Holt, 1995.

Woocher, Jonathan. *Sacred Survival: The Civil Religion of American Jews.* Bloomington: Indiana University Press, 1987.

———. "Toward a 'Unified Field Theory' of Jewish Continuity." New York: Jewish Education Service of North America, 1994.

Yapko, Benjamin L. "Jewish Elementary Education in the United States: Colonial Period to 1900." Ph.D. diss., American University, 1958.

Zeldin, Michael. "A Century Later and Worlds Apart: American Jews and the Public School–Private School Dilemma, 1870, 1970." American Jewish Archives, SC-13885. Los Angeles, 1986.

———. "Integration and Interaction in the Jewish Day School." In *The Jewish Educational Leader's Handbook,* ed. Robert E. Tornberg, 579–90. Denver: A.R.E., 1998.

———. "The Promise of Historical Inquiry: Nineteenth-Century Jewish Day Schools and Twentieth-Century Policy." American Jewish Archives Small Collections–13885. Los Angeles, 1987.

———. "What Makes a Reform Day School Reform?" Paper delivered to first Reform day school conference, Los Angeles, January 18, 1987. American Jewish Archives, SC-11031.

Zibbell, Charles. "Federations, Synagogues and Jewish Education in the 70s." *Jewish Education* 43, no. 3 (fall 1974): 40–45.

Zipperstein, Steven J. *Elusive Prophet: Ahad Ha'am and the Origins of Zionism.* Berkeley: University of California Press, 1993.

Zola, Gary P. "Jewish Camping and Its Relationship to the Organized Camping Movement in America." In *A Place of Our Own: The Rise of Reform Jewish Camping in America,* ed. Michael M. Lorge and Gary P. Zola, 1–26. Tuscaloosa: University of Alabama Press, 2006.

Index

B

bar/bat mitzvah courses and cere-
    monies, 14, 81, 96–97
  adult, 106
  celebration of, 28
  preparation for, 13, 45, 51
Bardin, Shlomo, 92
Baron, Salo, 116–17
Behrman House Publishers, 88–89, 90
Belkin, Samuel, 71
Benderly, Samson, 52, 58, 137n181
  educational camping and, 64–65,
    92, 138n199
  educational initiatives and pro-
    grams, 53, 59–60
  educational theories, 76
  Kaplan, Mordecai and, 55–56,
    58–59
Benderly boys, 58–59, 137n177
Berkowitz, Henry, 43
Beth Elohim synagogue, 11, 33
Beth Hayeled (House of the Child),
    72–73
Beth Jacob (Bais Yaakov) girls
    schools, 76
Bible, teaching of, 40, 135n142
Bible Ethics, 43
Bingham, Theodore A., 49–50
Birthright program, 101–2, 121
B'nai B'rith, 25–26
boarding schools, 29, 103
Board of Delegates of American Is-
    raelites, 132n100
Board of Teachers License, 58
boards of Jewish education. *See* bu-
    reaus of Jewish education
Boston Bureau of Jewish Education,
    66–67
Boston Hebrew Teachers College. *See*
    Hebrew Teachers College of
    Boston
Brandeis Camp Institute, 92
Brickner, Barnett, 58, 89

Brickner, Rebecca Aaronson. *See*
    Aaronson, Rebecca
bureaus of Jewish education, 6–7, 55.
    See also under individual city
    names
  founding and functions of, 51–52
  teacher training and, 121

C

CAJE. *See* Coalition for the Advance-
    ment of Jewish Education
    (CAJE)
Camp Achvah, 64–65, 92
Camp Cejwin, 64, 91
Camp Massad, 92
Camp Modin, 64
Camp Ramah, 92–93, 143n301
Camp Yavneh, 92
camp programs. *See* summer camp
    programs
Carlebach, Shlomo, 91
Carvalho, Emanuel N., 14, 128n33
Catechism for Younger Children, 18,
    20–21, 129n58
Central European Jews. *See* German
    Jews
Central Jewish Institute, 64, 91
Chabad-Lubavitch. *See* Lubavitcher
    (Hasidic) schools and outreach
    programs
charity schools, 13, 15
Chautauqua Society, 43. *See also* Jew-
    ish Chautauqua Society
Chazan, Barry, 104
children's literature. *See* literature,
    children's
Christian influence, 17, 44
  countering, 19, 30, 74
  in public education, 22–23, 38
Christian schools, 16–17
church-state separation, 63, 122
Coalition for the Advancement of Jew-
    ish Education (CAJE), 98, 120

Jewish Theological Seminary (JTS), 47–49. *See also* Teachers Institute (T.I.) of the Jewish Theological Seminary
founding of, 134*n*141, 135*n*143
library, 71
Jewish Welfare Board (JWB), 63–64. *See also* Janowsky Report (Oscar Janowsky)
JIR. *See* Jewish Institute of Religion (JIR)
Josephson, Manuel, 15
JTS. *See* Jewish Theological Seminary (JTS)
Judaism
Christianity and, 75, 90, 107–8
communal versus individual, 112, 146*n*357
distinctiveness of, 39–40, 44, 55, 80, 102
loss of, 94
Judaism as a Civilization, 73
Judaization, 94–95, 123. *See also* Americanization
JWB. *See* Jewish Welfare Board (JWB)

K
Kaplan, Mordecai, 46, 53
Benderly, Samson and, 55–56, 58–59
educational approaches, 73–74
egalitarianism and, 96–97
Teachers Institute (T.I.) of the Jewish Theological Seminary and, 49, 55
Kaplan-Cronson survey, 50–52
kehillah movement, 50. *See also* New York Kehillah
kiruv (drawing near). *See* outreach programs
Kley, Eduard, 20
Kohler, Kaufmann, 34, 70
Kohut, Alexander, 48

kolellim (programs of study for adults), 90–91, 111
Kotler, Aaron, 90
Krasner, Jonathan, 4, 44
Kvutzah (Camp Achvah), 64–65

L
Labor Zionists, 62. *See also* Zionism and Zionists
leadership
educational, 14, 17, 71, 109
opportunities for, 32–34
training for, 48, 52–54, 85, 92
Leaders Training Fellowship (LTF), 92
League of Jewish Youth, 58
learning, adult. *See* adult education; Jewish education: seniors
Leeser, Isaac, 17–18, 20–21, 129*n*49, 132*n*99
Levinger, Lee, 74–75
Levy, Isadore Montefiore, 63
libraries, Jewish, 30, 71
Liebman, Charles, 8, 97
Lilienthal, Max, 38
literary associations. *See* Jewish community centers
literature, children's. *See also* textbooks, Jewish
books, 72
periodicals, 38
Lookstein, Haskel, 72
Lookstein, Joseph, 72, 83
Los Angeles Bureau of Jewish Education, 113–14
LTF. *See* Leaders Training Fellowship (LTF)
Lubavitcher (Hasidic) schools and outreach programs, 76, 91, 105

M
Machzikei Talmud Torah Society, 30–31
Magnes, Judah, 50, 53